EGYPTIAN ARABIC
EASY STORIES WITH ENGLISH TRANSLATIONS

EGYPTIAN ARABIC

EASY STORIES WITH ENGLISH TRANSLATIONS

Donovan Nagel

Paperback Edition January 5, 2019
ISBN 978-1-7329287-0-1

Dedicated to Eman (aka Emma).

ABOUT TALKINARABIC.COM

TalkInArabic.com is the leading online resource for learners of spoken Arabic. Launched in 2014, it has quickly become the largest and fastest growing online platform, teaching 8 different dialects of colloquial Arabic with tens of thousands of active users worldwide.

For more information, visit:
www.talkinarabic.com

Contents

Introduction ii

How To Use This Book iv

عيلَة 1

وَجبَة مُميَّزة 9

ناس مَوهوبَة 19

يوم خروج الأم 27

إيطاليا 41

أسوأ يوم في المَدرَسة 55

نَوَّرت البيت 69

هَدَف 87

ياه، يا دُكتور 105

فُرصَة ذَهبيّة 121

حَظ وِحش 135

اليوم المُنتَظَر 151

Translations 167

Listen 203

INTRODUCTION

Most of the learning material and literature that currently exists for Arabic is written in and focused on teaching Modern Standard Arabic (MSA for short). This is the formal, standardized dialect which is used in most forms of Arab media, education and politics.

This has always been problematic for students of Arabic however, since MSA is a formal dialect that is not spoken by anyone as a native language. Students have often expressed great frustration when travelling to the Middle East or North Africa after studying a course in MSA, only to discover that they cannot communicate effectively with most people.

TalkInArabic.com and this series of short stories exists to provide *natural* Arabic learning material in the dialect that people communicate in every day.

It must be noted from the outset that it is generally very uncommon for Arabs to write in spoken dialects as this book has done. This makes it exceptionally difficult for learners of spoken varieties like Egyptian to acquire adequate and suitable reading material for learning.

Egyptian Arabic: *Easy Stories With English Translations* is a carefully crafted collection of simplified short stories written in the spoken vernacular of Egypt with corresponding English

translations. This book has been put together to help improve your comprehension in Egyptian Arabic while also helping you to boost your vocabulary.

This collection of easy stories has been tailored for Upper Beginner-level learners who are looking for challenging, fictional material to read in the spoken Egyptian variety of Arabic. We hope you'll find these stories both interesting and useful for your learning.

NOTE

This book assumes that you have *already* covered the basic fundamentals of the Arabic language. This means that you should already be able to read the alphabet and have a grasp of simple, core vocabulary typically taught in most beginner-level courses.

There is no transliteration in this book. You will find *taškīl* (vowel markings) but these have been used sparingly to assist in pronunciation. Where vowels are easily predictable by the reader, they've been left out.

If you are an absolute beginner and unacquainted with Egyptian Arabic, then we highly recommend returning to this book after covering the rudimentary aspects of the language.

HOW TO USE THIS BOOK

In this book you'll find 12 short stories in Egyptian Arabic that incrementally rise in length and difficulty.

The first 3 stories: Easiest and shortest.

The next 3 stories: Longer and more challenging.

The final 6 stories: The longest and most challenging.

At the end of each story, we've included a list of vocabulary along with comprehension questions to challenge your understanding of the text. Full English translations can be found at the very end of the book.

To get the most out of this material, we strongly advise refraining from referring to the English translations until you've completed the book or it's absolutely necessary. You should attempt to deduce the meaning from the immediate context first and when stuck, highlight the part (or utilize the ruled pages we've included) and move on. Often just knowing more of the story can boost your comprehension and help you to piece it all together. Make note of new expressions and vocabulary for later study.

Remember that repetition is key to learning Arabic. *Read often.*

1

عيلَة

أنا إسمي فاطِمة وعَندِي تَمَن سِنين.

عايشة فِي بيتي مع مَامَا وبَابا، وأخُويا الصُغير أمِير.

أمِير عَندُه سنة وَاحدة بس، وبيحِب يلعب مَعَايا.

النَهارده الصُبْح شِيلت أمِير لحد السُفرَة عشان الفطار، وبَابا إدَّاني شُويّة مِن القهوة بِتاعتُه.

أنا قُلت "يع"، وبَابا ضِحِك عليّا.

بَابا بِيِشْرَبْ قَهوة كُل يُوم عَلَى الفِطار، بس أنا

بَحِسّ إن رِيحِتْها وِحْشَة وِطَعمَها أوحَش.

مَامَا بِتِسْأَلْني: "عَايزَة مُرَبَّي عَلَى العِيش بِتَاعِك يا فَاظْمَة؟"

قُلْتِلها: **"أيوَة لَو سَمَحْتي، وأمير كَمَان عَايز شُويّة!"**

مَامَا قَالِتْ: **"حاضير"**، وحَطَّتْ شُويّة عِيش عَلَى طَبَق لِيَّا ولِأُخُويا.

لَمَّا مَامَا جَابِتْ لِنَا الطَّبَق، شُفْت أَمِير بِيلعَب بالعِيش بِتَاعُه بَدل مَا يَاكُله وذَا ضَحَّكْني.

بَابا إدّانَا كُلِّنَا بُوسَة وَرَاح الشُّغْل، وأنا فِضِلَت مَعَ أمير عَلى السُفرة نَاكُل فطارنَا.

أَمِيربيجِب يَبْهِدِل الدُّنْيا، ومَامَا بتِنَضَّفْ وَرَاه.

وأنَا بَفْضَل أضْحَك ومَامَا بِتِمْسَح المُرَبَّى مِنْ عَلَى خَدُّه.

خَلَّصْت الفِطار وخَرَجْت أَلْعَب مَعَ صَحْبِتي. لَازِم أَمَشِي لِآخِر الشَّارِعْ عشان أوصَّل لِصَحبِتي حَوَّاء.

شَعرها إسْوِد وعِينيها بُني زَيِّي، بَس هِيَّ أطْوَل مِيني بِكتير.

2

لمَّا وَصَلتْ لِبيتِهَا، أخُوهَا الكِبِير رَحَّب بِيا بابتِسَامَة كِبيرَة عَلى وِشّه.

وقالِّي: **"أهلًا يا فَاظْمَة."**

قلتله: **"أهلًا."**

سَألِني: **"عايزة حَوَّاء؟"**

قلته: **"أيْوة، عَايزة أشُوف لو هِيَّ عَايزة تِلعَب مَعَايا."**

نَادى بِصَوْت عَالِي: **"حَوَّاء!"**

رَدت وهِيَّ بتجري عَلى البَاب: **"جَاية."**

"صَباح الخِير يا حَوَّاء. عَايزة تِيجِي تِلعَبي معَايا؟"

قَالت و هِيَّ بتبتسم فِي وِشِي: **"أيْوة، يَاريِت."**

عَملنَا باي باي لأخُوهَا الكِبير، وجرِينَا عَلى الشَّارِع.

الدُّنيا شمس بَرَّه، ولَقِينَا كُورِتنَا اللي بِنلعَب بِيها. الشَّارِع مَليان نَاس، وأطفَال بِيلعَبُوا. أنا وحَوَّاء فضِلنَا نشُوط الكُورة لِبعَض تقرِيبًا طُول النهار.

3

دَيمًا بنِتبِسِط كتِير لمَّا نِلعَب مَعَ بعَض، وبتضَايق لمَّا يبقى لازِم أرجَع البيت.

لمَّا رِجِعتْ البيت أمِير نَام بِسُرعَة، وشُفت مَامَا بَدأت تِعمل عِيش فِي المَطبَخ.

سَألتهَا: **"أقدر أساعدِك؟"**

قَالِت لي: **"طبعًا"**، وإدتِني طَبَق كِبِير ومَعلَقة.

فِي الطَّبَق بِنْحُط الدِّقِيق والمَيه، وأنَا بَخلِطهُم مَعَ بعَض.

قَالِت لِي: **"بَابا هِيجِب ياكُل العِيش بِتَاعُه طَازه لمَّا يِجِي البيت."**

قُلت لها: **"عَشان يَاكلُه مَع قَهوة برِيحَة."**

ضِحكت لي، ووَرِتِني إزاي أكمل العيش.

أنَا بَحِب أعمِل العيش مَع مَامَا، وبَاكُل أول رغِيف لمَّا يِستِوِي.

بحِس إن أول واحد دَايمًا بيبقى طَعْمُه أحلَى.

4

Vocabulary

فطار	breakfast	سفرة	table
أسرَة	family	إبْتِسامَة	smile (noun)
شَال	to carry	شاوِر	to wave
جِري	to run	لِقي	to find
ضَحَك	to laugh	إنْبَسَط	to have fun
ريحَة	smell (noun)	ساعِد	to help
طَعْم	taste (noun)	سُلْطَنِيَة	bowl
مِربّى	jam	مَعلَقَة	spoon
بُوسة	kiss (noun)	خَلَط	to mix
مَسَح	to wipe	خَلَص	to finish
نَضَّف	to clean	فَوضى	mess
خَدّ	cheek	وَرّى	to show
لعب	to play	رِغيف	loaf

5

جاوِب بِصَح أو غَلَظ:

أ) فاطمَة بِتاكُل العَشا مَعَ عيليْها

ب) الدُنْيا بِتمَطَرْ بَرَّة

ت) فاطمَة عَنْدَها صاحْبَة اسْمَها حَوّا

ث) فاظْمَة عَندَها ثَمَن سِنين

ج) حَوّا قُصيِّرَة وشَعْرَها بُنّي

كَمِّل الجُمَل:

أ) فيه .... عَلَى حُدود أمير.

ب) فاطمَة حَطّت .... و .... في الطَبَق.

ت) أبوهُم .... كُل يوم قَبل الشُغل.

ث) فاطمَة زَعْلانَة عَشان لازِم ....

إخْتار الإِجابة الصَّح:

١.   الأَطْفال بيلعَبوا كورَة فين؟

   أ)   في المُنتَزَه العام.

   ب)   في بيت حَوّا.

   ت)   في الشارِع.

٢.   فاطمَة عايشَة مَعَ مين؟

   أ)   أبوها وأمّها.

   ب)   أمّها، أبوها، وأخوها الصُّغيّر.

   ت)   أمّها، أبوها، أخوها وأختَها.

٣.   مين بياكُل العيش الأوِّل؟

   أ)   أم فاطمَة.

   ب)   أبو فاطمَة مَعَ قَهوِتُه.

   ت)   فاطمَة.

NOTES

NOTES

2

وَجبَة مُميَّزة

النَهارِدَة عِيد مِيلَاد سَمِيرة، عَشَان كدا قَرَّرِتْ تعزِم أُسرتها عَلى العَشا فِي مطعمها المُفضَّل.

مطعم سَمِيرة المُفضَّل هُوَّ مطعم شاورما قُرَيِّب مِن بِيتِها، عَشان كِده هِيَّ قَالت لازم يِمشُوا لحد المطعم.

سَمِيرة عَندَها أُسرَة صُغَيَّرَة؛ جُوزها أسعد، ووِلَادْهَا عُمَر وإيمَان.

عَندُهُم خَمَسْ سنين وسنتين، وعشان كِده لازم تاخُد عربية الأطفَال لإيمَان.

لمَّا وَصَلوا لِلمطعم عُمر جِري عَلى ترَابيزة

جَمْب الشِبّاك.

هُوَّ بِيحِب التَرابيزة دِى أكتَر، عشان بِيعرف يِشُوف الجِنينَة اللي بَره.

أسعد شَال إيمَان مِن العربية وقَعدها على كُرسِي مَخصُوص، عَشان تطُول التَرابيزة زي أخُوها.

الجرسُون سأل: **"عَايزِين تَاكُلُوا إيه الليلَة دي؟"**

هُوَّ مَعاه وَرَقة وقلَم عشان يِكتِب كُل حَاجَة.

إيمَان قالت بِصُوت عَالي: **"عيش"**، وسَقِّفِت بِإيدِيهَا.

عُمَر قال: **"طعمية لو سمَحت."**

سَمِيرة قَالِت: **"عَاوزِين حَاجَة وِصَّاية لو سمَحت."** هِي بِتحِب كُل الأكَلات هِنا.

الجرسُون قال: **"حَاضِر، مِش هيطَوِّل. تِحبُّوا أجيبلُكُم عصير؟"**

سَمِيرة قالت: **"أَيوة من فضلك، كُلنا هناخُد عصير."**

سَمِيرة بِتحِب المطعم ده جِدًا، عشان كَانِت مِتعَوِدة تِيجِي هِنا لمَا كَانِت صُغِيرة، مامتها

كَانِت بِتأكّلْها عيش بالحُمّص.

سَميرة برضُو كَانِت بتاخد حِته مِن أكل كُل واحِد، عشَان ماكِنِتش بِتعرف تِختَار أكّلها المُفضَّل.

ودِلوَقتى بِما إنّها كبِرت بِتخلِي ولاذَها ياكلُوا اللي هُمَّا عَايزِينُه.

إيمَان صُغِيرة عَلى إنّها تَاكُل أكْل كتِير، عَشَان كِده هِيَّ بِتَاكُل عيش وحُمص زي سَمِيرة مَا كَانِت بِتَاكُل.

وكمَان بِتشرَب العَصِير؛ اللِي هُوَ أحسَن حَاجَة عندَها.

عُمَر بيِجب يَاكُل الطَّعْمِيّة جِدًّا، وهُوَ أول واحِد بِيخلَّص العَشَا؛ عشَان هُوَّ بِيَاكُل بِسُرعَة جِدًّا.

أسعد بِيِجب يسِيب سَمِيرة تِختَار له، عشَان هُوَّ بِيِجب يخلِّي سَمِيرة مبسوطة.

الجرسُون قال: **"اتفَضلوا العصير"**، وإدَّى كُل واحِد العصير بتاعه.

سَمِيرة قَالِت: **"شُكرًا"**، وسَاعدِت إيمَان تشرب شُوَيَّة.

عُمَر قال: **"مَامَا، أنا لِعبت مَع محمد فِي**

13

المَدرسة النَهاردَة."

قالت لُه: "جَمِيل، لِعبُوا إيه؟"

قَال: "استُغُمَّايَة. محمد بيعرف يستخبَّى كوَيِّس أوي."

أسعد قَال و هُوَّ بِيبِتِسِم لِعُمَر: "إنتَ كمان بتعرف تستخبَّى كوَيِّس."

اِبتَسِم هُوَّ كمَان لباباه. أسعد هُوَّ اللِي علَّمُه إزاي يلعَب استُغُمَّايَة، وبَعدَها عُمَر علَّم صُحَابه.

أكتَر حاجَة بِيحِبِّها فِي اللعبة هِيَّ العَدّ لِخَمسِين وصُحَابُه بِيستَخَبُّوا.

لمَّا الأكل وصَل كُل وَاحِد بدأ ياكُل، واتكَلِّمُوا عَن كُلّ حَاجَة عَمَلُوها فِي اليُوم دَه.

سَمِيرة فِضِلت فِي البِيت مَع إيمَان، وقَروا قِصَص.

أسعد رَاح الشُّغل، وكَان مشغُول جِدًا طُول اليُوم.

عُمَر رَاح المَدرسة مَع صُحَابه، واستَمتَعُوا كُلُّهم. الأكل لِذِيذ جِدًا، وبيتَّاكِل بِسُرعَة جِدًا.

14

سَمِيرة إتفاجِئِتْ جدًا لمَّا أسعد والوِلَاد فَاجؤوهَا بالهَدايا، وغنُّوا أُغنِيّة عِيد المِيلَاد.

سَمِيرة بِتحِب المطعم ده، عشَان بِيخَلِّي أُسرِتها سَعِيدة، وهِيَّ بِتحِب أُسرِتها جِدًا.

Vocabulary

عِيد مِيلَاد	birthday	قَرَّر	to decide
مُفضَّل	favorite	جِنِينَة	garden
مَطعم	restaurant	شِبَّاك	window
عَشاء	dinner	بَره	outside
شاورما	shawarma	مَخصُوص	special
حُمّص	hommus	صَفَّق	to clap
سَرَق	to steal	جرسُون	waiter
عصير	juice	إستَخَبّا	to hide
طَعمِية	falafel	عَدّ	counting
عِيش	bread	غَنَّى	to sing
عَرَبية	pram/stroller	مُفَاجَأة	surprise
استُغُمَّاية	hide and seek	أُغنِيّة	song
تزَابيزة	table	حِتّة	piece

جاوِب بِصَح أو غَلَظ:

أ)   دِي أوِل مَرّة سَميرَة تْروح المَطْعَم دَه.

ب)   إيمانْ بِتْحِب تِشرَب عَصيرْ.

ت)   العيلَة بِتُقْعُد عَنْد ظَرابيزَة في الجِنينَة بَرّة.

ث)   أشعَد قَعَد في البيتْ وقَرا قِصَص مَعَ إيمانْ.

ج)   عُمَر بيعْرَف يعّد لِخَمسين.

كَمِّل الجُمَل:

أ)   الكُل شِرِب .... مَعَ وَجِبتُه.

ب)   أم سَميرَة أكِلِتها .... و ....

ت)   .... بيعْرَف يستَخَبّى كوِيس جِدًا.

ث)   عُمَر بيحِب يبُص بَرَة عَلَى ....

إخْتار الإجابة الصَّح:

١. الأطْفال عَندُهُم كام سَنَة؟

أ) سَنَة وسِت سِنين.

ب) سَنَتين وخَمَس سِنين.

ت) سَنَتين وتَمَن سِنين.

٢. عُمَر لِعِب إيه في المَدرَسة النَهارْدَة؟

أ) كوزَة.

ب) إسْتُغُمّاية.

ت) غَد.

٣. سَميرَة مِتفاجِئَة ليه؟

أ) الأكل كان حِلو.

ب) عَشان خَدِت هَدايا.

ت) عشان خَدِت هدايا وغَنولهَا أغنية عيد ميلاد.

NOTES

NOTES

3

ناس مَوهوبَة

أنا إسمِي أمل، وهِوَايتِي المُفضَّلة هِيَ الرسم والتلوين.

أنا بِحِب أرسم وألوِّن كُل حَاجَة.

لوحتِي المُفضَّلة هِيّ اللي رَسَمتها لأَفْرَاد أُسرتي.

رسمت نفسِي، واخواتِي البنات الكُبار وبَابا قُدَّام بِيتْنا.

أنا بِحِب أستخدِم اللون الأزرَق كِتير لمَّا برسِم، عَشان هُوَّ لونِي المُفضَّل.

هُوَّ زَيْ السَّمَا.

أنا بِحِب أرسِم كُل يُوم تقريبًا، ورسم الحيوائات

هُوَّ أكتَر حاجَة بَحبَّها.

النَّهاردة هرسِم جمَل أصفر، مع رملة بُنِّي وسما زرقة كِبِيرة.

بتمنى كُل النَّاس تحب رُسومَاتِي.

فِي يُوم مِن الأيَّام أتمنى إني أرسِم لُوحة كِبِيرة عَلى الحِيطة زي اللي بشُوفهُم فِي الشَّوَارِع.

أنا عَايزة أخلِّي النَّاس سعيدة برُسومَاتِي.

عندِي صاحِب اسمُه محمد، وهُوَّ بيحِب يُطبُخ!.

لمَّا بزُورُه، دايمًا بيُطبُخ لِي.

سألتُه: **"هتُطبُخ إيه النهاردة يا محمد؟"**

قَال وهُوَّ بيخلِط الأكل: **"النهاردة هعمل تبولة."**

بحِب أشُوف محمد بيُطبُخ، لكِن اللي بحِبُّه أكتَر هُوَّ إني أكُل الأكل اللي عملُه.

أُم محمد بتعَلِّمُه إزاي يُطبُخ حَاجَات كِتِير مُختلِفة، وهُوَّ بيسَاعِدها فِي عمَايل العشَا كُل يُوم.

أعتقد إن الموضُوع مُمتِع جِدًا إنك تِبقَى قَادِر تُطبُخ كُويِس أوِي زِي صدِيقِي محمد.

صاحِبتنا أنجِلِينَا كُويسة جِدًّا فِي لعبِة كُورِة السَلَّة وهِيَّ بتسَاعِدِني عشَان أتعلِّمهَا.

أنا مِش كُويسة زيَّها فِي اللِعبة، بس هِيَّ بتلعب طُول الوَقت عشَان تِبقَى أحسَن كمَان.

أعتَقِد إنها فِي يُوم مِن الأيَّام هتِبقَى كُويسة بمَا فِيه الكِفَايَة إنها تِكسَب مَاتش مَع فرِيق مُمَيز!.

أنجِلِينَا قَالِت: **"أكثر حَاجَة بحِبَّهَا فِي لعبِة كُورِة السلة هِيَّ لحظَة رمْي الكُورة فِي السلة."**

ورتِني إزَّاي أرمِي الكُورة جَوَّه السلة، لكِن أنا مِش عَارفَة أعمِلهَا لِسه.

قالِت لِي: **"أخَدت وَقت كِبير عشَان أعرَف أعمِلهَا فِي البِدايَة أنا كمَان، بس لو فضِيلتي تحاولِي؛ فِي يُوم مِن الأيَّام هتِعرفِي تِعملِيهَا."**

أَنا سَعِيدَة إني عَندي صَديقة طيبة كِده.

عندِنا صديق بيجِب يعزف جِيتَار، واسمُه شَادِي.

إحنَا بنجِب نِسمع شَادِي وهُوَّ بيعزِف عَلى الجِيتَار بِتَاعُه، وساعات بنغنِّي شُوية أغَانِي مَعَاه.

شَادِي شَاطِر جِدًّا فِي العزف عَلى الجِيتَار، وبيعرَف يعزِف أغانِي كِتير.

شَادِي بيقُول إن باباه علّمه إزاي يعزِف، وإدالُه الجِيتَار بِتَاعُه فِي عِيد مِيلَادُه.

دِلوقِتِي شَادِي بَقى عندُه الجِيتَار بِتَاعُه، وبيجِيبُه معَاه فِي أَمَاكِن كِتِير ويعزِف مُوسِيقَى لكُل أصحَابُه.

رَغم إنَّا كُلِنَا عندِنَا هِوايَات مُختَلِفة، بس إحنَا أحَسن أصحَاب!.

بِنحِب نِتعلِم عن هِوايَات بعض. مُمتِع إنك تِتعلِم حَاجَات جِدِيدة.

بتمنى بِجد مبَطَّلش أبدًا أتعلَّم حَاجَات جدِيدة.

Vocabulary

Arabic	English	Arabic	English
هِوَاية	hobby	شَارِع	street
لوحَة	painting	طَبَخ	to cook
رَسم	drawing	تَبُولَة	tabbouleh
لون	color	فَنّ	art
أزرَق	blue	كُورة السِلّة	basketball
رَسَم	to paint	رَمى	to throw
سمَاء	sky	كُورة	ball
حَيوان	animal	سَلّة	hoop
أصفر	yellow	حَاوِل	to try
جمَل	camel	جِيتَار	guitar
بُنّي	brown	سَمَع	to listen
رَملَة	sand	مُختَلِفة	different
حِيطة	wall	مَكان	place

جاوِب بِصَح أو غَلَظ:

أ)   مِحَمَّد اتْعَلَّم يُطْبُخ لِوَحْدُه.

ب)   لُون إيمان المُفَضَّل هُوَ البَنَفِسِجي.

ت)   أبو شادي عَلِّمُه يِلعَب التشيلُو.

ث)   أمَل بِتِلعَب كُرة سلّة أحسَن مِن أنْجِلينا.

ج)   النَهاردَة أمَل هتلَوِّن جَمَل بُنّي.

كَمِّل الجُمَل:

أ)   أمَل .... صُورَة عيلِتها .... بيتهُم.

ب)   مِحَمَّد بيتعَلَّم .... مِن أمُّه.

ت)   أمَل مَبِتعرَفش .... كورَة في .... لغاية دِلوَقتي.

ث)   .... بيلعَب موسيقَى لِكُل ....

إخْتار الإجابة الصَّح:

١. إيه رَسمِة أمَل المُفَضَّلَة؟

أ) جَمَل.

ب) حَيَوانات.

ت) عيلِتها.

٢. مِحَمَّد هَيُطبُخ إيه النَهارَدَة؟

أ) فِراخ.

ب) تَبولَّة.

ت) عيش.

٣. مين اشتَرَى جيتار لشادي؟

أ) صاحبُه المُفضَّل.

ب) أمُّه.

ت) أبوه.

NOTES

Notes

4

يوم خروج الأم

دِي نَادِيَة، والنهَاردة هَيكون يُوم مُمتِع بِالنسبة لها.

مَعزُومة عَلى فَرَح صَاحِبتها، ومِحتَاجة فُستَان حلو تِلبِسُه.

نَادِيَة وصَاحِبتها يعرفوا بعض من وهمَّا صغيرين جِدًا، عشَان كِدَة هِيَّ فرحانة جِدًا لصَاحِبتها.

نَادِيَة مُتشَوقَة إِنها تِرُوح تشتري الحاجات، مِش بس عشَان هتشُوف صَاحِبتها التَانية، لأ كمَان عشَان هتِسِيب العِيَال فِي البيت وتقَضِّي اليَوم لِنَفْسَهَا!.

نَادِية حطّت ماكياجهَا، ونزلت بَره تستنَّى صَاحِبِتها أميرة اللِيَ هتاخُدهُم لِلمُول.

عربِيتها ركِنِت، و نَادِيَة ركِبِت جمبَها.

نَادِيَة قالت لأميرة: **"أنا مُتَحَمِّسَة جِدًا."**

ردت أميرة وهي بتسُوق لِلمحَل: **"وأنا كمَان، العِيَال عَامِلِين إيه؟"**

قَالِت: **"مِش تمَام أوي، كَانُوا تعَبانِيِين طُول الأسبُوع، وأنا تقريبًا مكنتش بنام."**

أميرة قَالِت: **"مِش حلو كِدَه، أتمنى يبقُوا أحسن قُرِيب المسَاكِين دُول"**، وشغَّلِتْ الرَاديو.

الأصحَاب كانوا بيغنُّوا أغَانِيهُم المُفَضَّلة عشَان يسلُّوا وقتهم طُول المِشوار الظَويِل.

لمَّا وصلُوا لِلمحل قررُوا هُمَّا الاتنين يُروحُوا محل اللِبس الرسمِي الأول.

قَالِت نَادِيَة وهِيَّ مُتَحَمِسة: **"فِي خِيَارات كِتِير أوي"**

أميرة قَالِت: **"عَارفة. تُحَفَة صح؟"** هِيَّ بتحب الشوبِنج، وجريت عَلى أول رف فوزًا وبدأت تِتفرَج عَلى الفسَاتِين.

نَادِية سَألِت وهِيَّ بتضحَك: "أبدأ مِنين؟"

أميرة اقترحت: "طيّب، لِيه متبصّيش عَلى الألوَان اللِي بتحبّيهَا وتبتدِي مِن هِنَاك؟"

نَادِية راحِت للرف اللِي مِتعلّق علِيه فسَاتِين زرقة كِتِير.

الأزرق هُوَّ لُونهَا المُفَضّل؛ عشَان كِدَه قررِت تختار شُوِيّة عَلى مقاسها.

أميرة قَالِت: "يلا نرُوح نقِيس دُول"، وكانت مُتحَمّسة جِدًا ومعَاها حوالي خمَس فسَاتِين.

نَادِية وأميرة دخلُوا أُوض تغْيير اللِبس، وكُل واحدة جربِت أول فُستَان.

أميرة اختَارت فُستَان أحمر قُصير، ونَادِية اختَارت واحِد أزرق فَاتِح.

خرجُوا مِن الأُوض عشَان يفرجُوا بعض.

أميرة قَالِت لنَادِية: "عجبِني أوي دَه بجد، مُنَاسِب لِيكِي جدًا!"

نَادِية قَالِت: "أعتقِد بتاعِك قُصيَر شُوِيّة"، وزَاحُوا يجربُوا اخِتياراتهُم التَّانية.

المَرَّة دِي نَادِية جرِبِت فُستَان أزرق غَامِق يدُوب فوق رُكبِتهَا، وأميرة جربِت فُستَان وردِي بكشكشة عَلى الكتف.

أميرة مَاشية تِضحَك، عشَان الكشكشة بتخبط فِي وِشهَا.

قَالِت: **"شَكْلِي هبلة"**، ونَادِية وافقت عَلى كلامَها.

نَادِية بدأت تنبِسط وقالت وهِيَّ بِتضحَك: **"حَاسة إن الفُستَان دَه ينفع ألبِسُه فِي الشُغل، بَس مِش فِي فرح!"**

رجعُوا لأُوض تَغْيِير الملابس تَانِي، نَادِية لبِست أخِر فُستَان.

فُستَان طويل جِدًا، لدرجِة إنهَا خرجت بيه بصعُوبة.

أميرة لبِست فُستَان أخضر حِلو شبه لُون عِنيهَا.

نَادِية قَالِت: **"عَاجبِني دَه، مخلِّي عينِيكِي حلويين جِدًا!"**

أميرة قَالِت: **"شُكرًا، أعتقد أول واحد جربتِيه كَان هُوَّ أحلى واحد."**

نَادِية قَالِت: **"وأنا كمَان"**، وَراحُوا يغيِّرُوا مَرة تَانية ولبسُوا لبسُهُم العَادِي.

عند الكَاشير أميرة دفعِت تمن فُستَانها الأخضر، وقررِت كمَان تِشترِي سلسِلة فضي خبتَها مِن نَادِية.

نَادِية خدت أول فُستَان للكَاشير.

أميرة قَالِت: **"دلوقتِي محتَاجِين جِزَم!"**، وخذت نَادِية مِن إيدِيهَا عَلى المحل اللِي بعدُه.

نَادِية بتضحك، وكَانِت هتوقَّع شنطِتها.

قَالِت: **"بِرَّاحة."**

أميرة قَالِت: **"لأ، الجِزَم هِيَّ أحسن حَاجة بالنسبة لِي"**، ودخلُوا محل الجِزَم.

نَادِية اشتكت: **"مِش بحِب ألبِس كَعب عالِي."**

أميرة ردَّت: **"خلَاص، اختارِي مِن غِير كَعب."**

نَادِية قرَّرت تزُوح لرف الخُصُومَات، وتدور هِناك.

لقت جَزمَة رمادِي حلوة حسَّت إنَّها مُريحَة جِدًا، وقررِت تجِبهَا تِلبسهَا عشان لو هتجرِي وَرَا عِيالها طُول اليُوم.

أميرة سأَلِت: **"العِيال محتَاجِين جِزَم هُمَّا**

كَمَان؟"، وكانت مَاسكة صندل بنَاتِي جَمِيل.

"أووووه، أنَا مُتأكِدة إنه هيعجبها، شُكرًا!"، وأخِدِت الصندل لِبنتهَا.

وبِالنِسبة لِابنهَا قَررت تاخد جَزمَة سُودا كلاسِيك وأخِدِت كُل حَاجة للكَاشِير.

أميرة اختارِت صندل حرِيمِي أبيض بِكَعب عالِي.

نَادِية قَالِت: **"مقدَرش حتى أمِشي بِيه دَه."**

هُمَّا الاتنِين دفعُوا تمن الجِزَم، ونَادِية قَالِت الأَحسن تِختَار حَاجة للعِيَال يلبِسُوها هُمَّا كمَان.

لمَّا وصلُوا لِمحَل الأَطفَال نَادِية اختارِت فُستَان أبيض جمِيل لِبنتهَا، مِتخيِّط عليه شُوية ورد ملوَّن وزاهِي وده هِيخلِّي بِنتهَا تِفرح جِدًا.

لِابنهَا اختارِت تِي شِيرت شَبه جَاكِيت البدلة مِن فُوق، وبنظلُون جِينز إسوِد صُغير.

أميَرة قَالِت: **"شَكلُهُم هَيبقى تُحفَة."**

ضِحكِت نَادِية وقَالِت: **"تُحفَة أكتَر من شَكلُهُم الأسبُوع دَه؟؟، شَكلُهُم فظيع!"**

أميرة ضِحكِت وقَالِت: **"أتمني مايِعدُوكِيش قبل الفرح"**، واقترحت يِجيبوا قَهْوَة يشرَبُوهَا فِي

طريقهُم لِلبِيت.

نَادِية قَالِت: **"أعتقد إننا نِستحقّها"**، فرَاحُوا يطلُبوا القَهُوَة، وبعدين راحُوا عَلى العَربية.

أميرة قَالِت: **"أنا مُرهَقَة!"**

نَادِية قَالِت: **"وأنا كمَان، أتمنى العشَا يكُون جَاهز أول مَا أرجع البِيت، أنا جعَانة جِدًا!"**

أميرة قَالِت: **"هيكون كوَيّس جِدًا، الأحسن تسَلميلي عَلى العِيَال بقَى عشَان مِش عَايزاهم يعدوني!"**

نَادِية قَالِت: **"فِكرة كُويسَة، شُكرًا بجد إنك جِيتي معَايا النَهَاردة، أنا عادَة بَكرَه الشوبنج بس بجد كَان مُمتِع جِدًا معَاكِي!"**

أميرة قَالِت: **"العفو، أي وقت عَايزة حَد يجِي معَاكي أنا هَاجِي.   إنتِ عَارفة أد إيه بحب الشوبنج."**

نَادِية ضِحكِت وقَالِت: **"أشُوفِك فِي الفرح!"**

أميرة قَالِت: **"أشُوفِك هِنَاك!. تصبحي على خير، وأتمني العِيَال يبقُوا أحسَن وقتها"**، ونَزِّلت نَادِية قُدَّام بِيتها.

Vocabulary

شوبِنج	shopping	إتمَنّى	to hope
مُمتِع	fun	جعَانة	hungry
مَعزُومة	invited	إتسَلّا	to occupy/pass time
فرح	wedding	وَرد	flower
لبس	to wear	محل	shop
مُتشَوّقَة	to look forward to	قَرّر	to decide
مُرهَقَة	exhausted	رسمِي	formal
سآب	to leave (behind)	لِبس	clothes
ماكياج	makeup	إستَحَقّ	to deserve
زَكَّن	to pull up	حَسّ	to feel
رِكِب	to ride	رَقّ	shelf
سَاق	to drive	فُستَان	dress
دَفَع	to pay	إبتَدى	to start
إقتَرَح	to suggest	مُنَاسِب	suitable

Vocabulary

عَلَّق	to hang	تْغِيِير	change/transition
مَقَاس	size	أزرق غَامِق	dark blue
أُوضة تْغِيِير	change room	كِتف	shoulder
ناعِم	flowy	كشكشة	ruffles
قُصير	short	ورِدي	pink
وِش	face	عين	eye
هَبلة	ridiculous	عَادِي	normal
شُغل	work	فضي	silver
أبيض	white	سلسِلة	necklace
أخضر	green	خَبّى	to conceal
كَاشير	cashier	بِرّاحة	slowly
جِزَم	shoes	دَخُل	to enter
وَقَّع	to drop	كَعب عالي	high heels
إشتَكى	to complain	مُريحة	comfortable

39

VOCABULARY

غِير كَعب	flat (shoes)	صندل	sandals
رمادِي	grey	سُودا	black
إختَار	to choose	تِي شِيرت	t-shirt

جاوِب بِصَح أو غَلَظ:

أ)   أميرَة بِتِشتِري فُستان بَمُبي وعُقْد فَضّة.

ب)   ناذْيَة بِتِشتِري شوَيّة جِزَم رُصاصي.

ت)   ناذْيَة بِتِشتِري فُستان أزرَق غامِق.

ث)   السِت بِتِشْرَب عَصير وهُمَّ مِرَوَّحين البيت.

ج)   ناذْيَة بِتِكرَه شِرا الحاجات بَس أميرَة بِتْحِبْه.

كَمِّل الجُمَل:

أ)   السِتات بِتِسمَع .... وهي بِتتسوق.

ب)   .... كانوا تَعبانين طول ....

ت)   .... بِتِلِبِس .... أخضَر لايق عَلَى عيونها.

ث)   ناديَة بِتِشتِري .... و .... إسوِد لابنَها.

41

إخْتار الإجابة الصَّح:

١. إيه لون نادِيَة المُفضَّل؟

أ) أحمَر.

ب) أزرَق.

ت) أخضَر.

٢. إيه نوع المَحلَّات اللي البِنات بتروحُه الأوَّل؟

أ) مَحَّل لِبس أطفال.

ب) مَحَّل جِزَم.

ت) مَحَّل لِبس رَسمي.

٣. أيه التَصميم إللي عَلَى فُستان بِنت نادِيَة؟

أ) مَفيش تَصميم.

ب) نُقَط.

ت) وَرد.

NOTES

NOTES

5

إيطاليا

كَان صبح يُوم سبت دافي، و يُوسِف كَان مُتَحمِّس جِدًّا.

كَان فِي العربية في الطَرِيق للمظار لمُغَامرة مُثِيرَة.

يُوسِف وأُسرِته كانوا رايحِين أجَازة لإيطاليا!.

يُوسِف زار إيطاليا قبل كِدَه، بس كَان صُغَير جِدًّا ومش مُمْكِن يفتِكِر أي حَاجَة خالِص.

المرة دِي عندُه عشَر سِنِين، وهِيفتِكِر الرحلة للأبد.

باباه كَان بيسُوُق العربية، ومامته كَانِت بتغنِّي

مَع الراديُو.

يُوسِف كَان بيبُص مِن شِباك العربية عَلى العربيات التانية وهي بتعدِّي.

لمّا وصلُوا للمظار، نزّلُوا شُنطهُم وحطُّوها عَلى الترولِّي.

و بابا يُوسِف زَقْ الترولِّي لحد صالة الانتظار.

كَان لازم يطلَّعُوا جَوازَات سفرهُم وتذاكرهُم عند المكتّب.

يُوسِف حفظ أرقَام كَراسِي الطيارة، وكَان مُتَحمّس جِدًا عشَان يوصل لكُرسِيه.

كَانِت رحلة طيَران طويلَة ويُوسِف اتفرَّج عَلى الأرض وهِيَّ شكلَها صُغَيَّر جِدًا مِن شَبابِيك الطيَّارة.

وكَمَان اتفرَّج عَلى شُوية أفلَام عَلى تلفزيُون الطيارة الخَاص.

مامته نامِت شُوية لكِن يُوسِف كَان مُتَحمّس جِدًا لدرجة إنه مَعْرِفْش ينام.

وكَان بيفكَّر فِي كُل الحَاجَات المُمتِعَة اللِي مُمكِن يقدر يعملِها فِي الأجَازة.

لمَّا وصلُوا إيطاليا، كَان فِي أخِرِ النهَار، والأُسرة اتَّجَهِت مُباشرةً للفُندُق اللِي هيُعُدوا فِيه.

يُوسِف حب جِدًا السرِير النَاعِم الكِبير اللِي هينام عَليه، والتِلفزيُون الكِبير اللِي هيتفَرج عَليه، بس أكتر حَاجَة حبها هيَّ منظر الشَارِع الزحمة وكُل الألوَان الزاهِية اللِي شَايفها.

يُوسِف كَان مُتَحمِّس جِدًا عشَان يستكشف إيطاليا.

وكَانُوا مخطَّطِين كتِيرللمُغَامرة الكِبيرة؛ زي الأَكل اللِذِيذ، والخرُوج فِي جولَات سياحِية وزيارِة الأماكِن المشهُورة.

هَيبِعِدوا عَن البيت لمُدة أسبُوعِين كامِلِين!.

مامتُه قَالت: **"هات الجَاكِيت بتَاعك، إحنا خارجِين عشَان نتعشَى!"**

يُوسِف قَال **"جَي أُهوه!"**، وجرى يجِيب حَاجْته وسأل: **"إحنَا رايحِين فِين؟"**

باباه قَال: **"فِي مطعَم جمِيل فِي آخِر الشَّارِع"**، وبدأوا يمشُوا.

يُوسِف كَان قَادِر يشم رِيحِة الأَكْل حتى قبل ما يدخلُوا المبنى، وحَس إنه كَان جعَان جِدًا.

47

جرسُون شِيك جِدًا خدهُم للترَابِيزة، وقدم لهُم المنيو.

يُوسِف طلب طبق سباجتّي كبِير عليه جبنة كتِير عَلى الوِش، وللحلو طلب جِيلاتِي.

الأكل كَان لذِيذ أوي وخلّاهُم كُلهم مبسوطين جِدًا.

فِي اليُوم اللي بعدُه يُوسِف وباباه ومامته خرجُوا فِي جولة سياحِية فِي المدِينة اللِي كَانُوا قاعدِين فِيها.

كَانِت جولة مُمَيزة جِدًا؛ لإنهُم ركبُوا سكُوترَات كهربَائِية!.

وحتى يُوسِف كَان مسمُوح لُه يسُوق بتاعُه بنفسُه واتبسط جِدًا.

اتعلمُوا حَاجَات كتير عن المبانِي القدِيمة، اللِي اتبنت مِن أكتر مِن مِيت سنة، وبتاعِت ناس أغْنِيه جِدًا.

يُوسِف قعد يتخَيّل الغَني عامِل إزاي وإزاي بيعيش فِي بيت فخم كِدَه.

يوسِف قَال لِباباه: **"لو كُنت غِني زيهُم، كُنت هعيش مع كُل أصحابِي وبدل ما نرُوح المدرسة**

48

كُنا هنقعد نلعب ألعاب فِيديُو."

باباه قَال لُه: **"دا كَان هَيبقى مُمتِع أوِي!"**

مامته سَألته: **"هتعلّمني ألعَب ألعاب الفِيديو عشَان أعيش هِناك أنا كمَان؟"**

يُوسِف قَال لها: **"أيوة!"**، وكملوا مشي فِي الشوارع وهما بيسمعوا القصص.

فِي اليُوم اللِي بعد جولة السكُوتر بتاعتهُم، بابا يُوسِف و مامته خذُوه لمدِينة اسمها فينيسيا.

وكَانِت مكَان يُوسِف المُفضّل.

حبها جِدًا عشَان بدل الطُرق كَان عندهُم قنَوات كِبِيرة ملِيانة بالمية، وبدل العربِيَات كَان عندهم مراكِب.

فِي الجزء الخلِفِي مِن المركِب بيقُف راجِل ويجدّف بيهُم.

وعِرف يُوسِف إن المراكِب دِي كَان اسمهَا **"الجندول."**

وفِي اليُوم ده يُوسِف ركب جنادِيل كِتِير، وشَاف ناس كتِير لابسِين أقنِعة ولبس ملوِن.

ويُوسِف كان شايف إنُه مُمتِع جِدًا إنه يلبِس زيهُم بالزبط.

49

وكَانُوا بيغنُّوا ويرقصُوا ليُوسِف وهوَ كان مُستمتِع أوي.

يُوسِف سَأل: "مُمكِن أشترِي قِناع مِن دُول وأخذُه مغَايا عشَان أوريه لأصحَابِي؟"

مامتُه قالِت: **"فِكرة هايلة"**، وأخدِته عشان يختار قِناع.

ساعدِتُه فِي عد الفلُوس ويُوسِف اختار قِناع أحمر عليه ريش كتِير.

يُوسِف حب الريش الناعِم ومكنش قادِر يُصبر عشَان يوريه لأصحَابه فِي المدرسة ويحكيلهُم عن الفنانِين اللي شافهُم كُلهُم.

حاجة مسلية تانية يُوسِف عملهَا فِي أجَازته؛ هِيَّ إنه اتعلِّم إزاي يعمِل بيتزا!.

خذُوا درس خَاص لتعليم عمَايل البيتزا ويُوسِف اتعلم كُل حَاجَة عن الموضوع دَه.

أولًا إتعلِّم إزاي يعمِل العجينة، ويعجنها عَلى التَّرابِيزة.

وبعدِين الشيف علمهُم إزاي يدوّرُوا العجينة فِي الهَوا، ويلفوها بسرعة لحد ما تبقَى دايرة كِبيرة.

مامة يُوسِف وقَّعِت العجينة بتاعِتها عَلى الأرض، ويُوسِف وباباه ضِحكُوا عليها.

يُوسِف كَان دورُه بعدها وعملها كويس جِدًا، وكانِت على شَكل دايْرَة صُغيرة.

الشيف حط البيتزا عَلى الصَّنية، و يُوسِف حَظ عليها الإضافات المُفضَّلة ليه.

اختار صلصة الطمَاطِم، والببروِني، والمشروم، والفلفِل، وجبنة لذِيذة كتير جِدًا.

الشيف قَال: **"دلوقتِي هنحُظ البيتزا فِي الفُرْن."**

يُوسِف قَال: **"مِش قادِر أصبر عشَان أكُل البيتزا بتاعتِي."**

مامِتُه قَالِت: **"شَكلَها لذيذة أوي"**، وراحُوا قعُدوا عَلى تَرابيزة.

يُوسِف اتفرج عَلى البيتزا وهي بتستوي فِي الفُرْن الكبير لحد ما بقِت جَاهِزة للأكل.

الشيف طلَّعَها مِن الفُرْن وقدمها لهُم وقطعها شَرايِح.

الشيف قال بابتسامة كِبيرة: **"استمتِع بالبيتزا الجمِيلة بتاعتك."**

يُوسِف عمل حَاجَات كتير مُمْتِعَة فِي أجَازته

الكبيرة لإيطاليا، وكَان زعلان لمَّا جِه يركب الطيارة عشَان يرجع لبلدُه.

يوسِف سَأل باباه و مامتُه: **"مُمْكِن نيجِي لإيطاليا مرة تانْية فِي يُوم مِن الأيَّام؟"**

مامته قالت: **"طبعا!"**

باباه قَال: **"أَظُن إن دِي هَتكون حَاجَة جميلة."**

VOCABULARY

أجازة	holiday	دافي	warm
السبت	Saturday	راديُو	radio
صُبح	morning	بَصّ في	to look at
مُتَحمّس	excited	إتفَرّج عَلى	to watch
عربية	car	غَدّى	to go by
مطار	airport	وَصَل	to arrive
مُثِيرَة	exciting	نَزّل	to unload
مُغَامرة	adventure	شَنطة	bag
إفتَكَر	to remember	انتظَار	waiting
رِحلة	trip	بَسبور - جَوَاز سَفَر	passport
للأبد	forever	تَذكَرَة	ticket
طرِيق	road	مكتَب	desk
طويل	long	حَفظ	to memorize
كُرسِي	seat	إستَكشِف	to explore

53

Vocabulary

رَقَّم	number	جولة سياحِية	tour
طيارة	airplane	زَار	to visit
أرض	land	جَاكِيت	coat/jacket
فَكَّر	to think	منيو	menu
قَعَد	to stay	جِيلاتي	gelato
سرير	bed	مدِينة	town
ناعِم	soft	كهربَائِية	electric
زحمة	crowded	مسمُوح	allowed
بِتَاع	belongs to	جَدَّف	to paddle/row
إتخَيِيل	to imagine	قِنَاع	mask
لعب فِيديُو	video game	ملوِن	colorful
مَركِب	boat	رَقصَة	dance
وِقِف	to stand	رِيش	feather
فَنَّان	performer	بيتزا	pizza

VOCABULARY

عجينة	dough	عَجَّن	to knead
شيف	chef	دَوَّر	to toss(turn)
دَايرَة	circle	صينية	tray
إضافات	toppings	صلصة الطَمَاطِم	tomato paste
ببروني	pepperoni	مشروم	mushroom
فلفِل	capsicum	فُرن	oven
جَاهِزَة	to be ready	قَطَع	to chop/cut
فِلم	movie	جِبنَة	cheese
شَريحَة	slice	سكُوتر	scooter
فُندُق	hotel	مَبنى	building
غَنِي	rich	قَنَاة	canal

جاوِب بِصَح أو غَلَط:

أ) وَليد عَندُه ثَلاتين سَنَة وعَندُه سِت إخْوات ولاد.

ب) وَليد دائِمًا بِيشيل إزازة مَيّه في شَنْطِتُه.

ت) وَليد بيرْسِم في الرَمْل بِصابعُه/بِصْباعُه.

ث) الطُّلّاب بيبْعَتوا رَسايِل لِصُحابهُم اللّي مِن بَرّة في إنْجِلِترا.

ج) أسْعَد ضِحِك عَلَى وَليد.

كَمِّل الجُمَل:

أ) وَليد بيحِب .... عَشان هو بيفهَم إزاي يِتعامِل مَعَ الأرْقام.

ب) .... وَليد بِتقولُه يِفضَل يِحاوِل.

ت) الطُّلّاب عَندُهُم صُحاب أجانِب في ....

ث) .... وَليد بِتصُب .... شاي.

إخْتار الإجابة الصَّح:

١. إيه إللي خَلَّى يوم وَليد وِحِش جِدًا؟

أ)   إنّه بيكرَه حِصّة الرياضَة.

ب) إنُّه مَبيعرَفش يرسِم صُوَر.

ت) إن فيه وَلَد بيضحَك وبيرمي حاجات عَليه.

٢. في وَقت الغَدا، وَليد بيحاوِل يلاقي ...

أ)   مُدَرِّسته.

ب) مَكان هادي.

ت) قَلَم رُصاص.

٣. وَليد نِسي ياخُد إيه المَدرَسة؟

أ)   غَداه.

ب) إزازِة المَيّه بِتاعتُه.

ت) جَوابُه مِن سارة.

NOTES

NOTES

6

أسوأ يوم في المَدرَسَة

أنا إسمِي وليد، وعندِي تَلَتَّاشَر سنَة وعندِي ست إخوات.

كُلّنَا عَايشِين سوَا فِي بيِت صُغَير فِي شَارِع زحمَة.

النَهَاردة يُوم التلات الصُبح وأنا رايح المَدْرَسَة زِي مَا بعمِل كُل يُوم.

بِحِب أرُوح المدرسة عشَان أشُوف أصحَابِي، وأتعلِّم حَاجَات جدِيدة.

مادِتِي المُفضَّلة هِيَّ الرياضة.

سبب حُبِّي لِلرِّياضة أوي كِدَه؛ هُوَّ إنِّي بحِب أفهم طَرِيقة عمل الأرقَام، وطرِيقة كِتَابة المُعَادلات.

وكمَان بتسَاعِدني أتعلَّم أكتر عن الفلُوس.

باستمتِع بالمَشي لِلمَدرَسَة، عشَان بيدِيني شُوِية وَقت لِنفسِي بِعيد عن عِيلِتي الكبيرَة.

أعتقد إن النهَارده هَيْكون يُوم حَرّ لِأن الشمس حامِية فِعلًا عَلَى جِلدِي، وبدَأت أعطش فِعلًا.

هشرب مِن إزازة المِيَّه بتَاعِتي لمَّا أوصل المدرسة.

دايمًا بخلِّي مغَايا واحدة فِي شنطِتي.

الطريق للمدرسة طوِيل، عشَان كِدَه أنا لازِم أنزِل بدرِي وأمشِي فِي الشوَارِع الزحمَة.

لمَّا بوصل للمدرسة، برُوح عَلى فصلِي، وهُوَّ ضِيل ولطِيف من جُوَّه.

فتحت شنطِة الضهر بتَاعِتي عشَان أجيب إزازة المِيه بس ملقِتهَاش!.

اتضَايقت، وكُنتُ عَطشَان جِدًا.

قعدت عَلى الدسك واستنيت صَاحبِي يِجي.

زَمايْلي التَّانْيِين وصلُوا وقعدُوا عَلى دسكاتهم، بس صَاحِبِي مجَاش.

أعتقد أنه تعبَان، عشَان أسعد بيِجِب يِجِي المَدرَسَة زَيي.

النهَارده هكُون لوَحْدِي.

أسعد هُوَّ أكتَر واحِد صَاحبِي ومَلِيش أي أصحَاب تَانيِين، عشَان أنا جدِيد فِي المدرسة.

لمَّا المُدَرّسة وصلِت قَالِتلنا: يلا، هنقرأ، فكُلِنَا طلَّعْنَا كُتُبنَا عشَان نبدَأ نِقرَأ بالدُور بصوُت عَالِي.

لمَّا دُورِي جِه، ولد وَزَايَا ضحك علَيا عشَان عندِي صعُوبة فِي نُطق شُوية كلمَات.

بيضايقني جِدًا إن حد يضحك عَليَّا، وبيخَلِيني عَايز أوقَّف قِراية.

مُدَرّستي ابتَسَمت فِي وشِي وقَالِتلِي أفضل أحَاوِل، وأنا عَمَلت كِدَه.

لمَّا وصلت لِنِهَاية الجُزء بتَاعِي الولد ضِحك تَانِي، وأنا نِزِلْت تَحت الدسك بتَاعي.

الحِصة اللِي بعدهَا قرر الولد إنه يرمِي حَاجَات عَليا لمَّا المُدَرّسة مَكِنتش واخدة بَالهَا.

دَه ضايِقني جِدًا، وخلاّني خَايف أطلَع الفُسحَة أكُل غذَايا مَع باقِي الأولاد.

فحَاوِلت ألاقِي مكَان هَادِي أقعُد فِيه أكُل غذَايا، الأَكل مَلَى بطِني وخلاّني أحسن شوية.

كُنت أتمَنّى مَرجَعْش الفصل تَانِي، بس يِمكِن نَاخُد شوية رِيَاضة النهَارده.

وذَه هَيبسطني أعتَقِد.

فِي وقت الغذَا رسمت عَلى التُراب بعصَاية، عشَان مَكُنتِش لاقِي حاجة أعْمِلهَا.

أنا مِش كويِّس فِي رسم الصُور، بجِب أرسِم أشكَال ونماذِج.

أسعد صَاحْبِي شَاطِر فِي الصُور.

أتمنَّى يكُون هِنَا دِلوقتِي عشَان يرسِم معَايا.

بنرسِم غالبًا كُل يُوم مَعَ بعض بَعد ما نخلَّص أكل.

لمَّا رجِعنا الفَصل بعد الغذَا المُدرِّسة قَالِتلِنا إنَّا هنكتِب رِسالَة لأصدقاء المراسلة.

إحنَا نعرف فصل طُلاب زينَا بالزبْط بس عَايشِين فِي أمريكا، وبنزَّاسِل بعض عَلَطُول.

ده بيسَاعِدنَا عَلى مُمارِسة الكِتابَة بالانجليزِي، وبرده مُمتِع إنَّا نكوّن صَداقات جِديدَة.

صديقْتي فِي المُراسَلة اسمهَا سَارة، فكتبتلها رِسَالة وحكِيتلَها عَن يُومِي.

وقررت أقُولهَا عن مِشْوَاري للمدرسة، وإزاي باستَمتِع بالوقَت بعِيد عن أُسرتي.

أُسرتي وحْشَاني دِلوقْتي عشَان أنا حاسِس بالوِحدة.

لمَّا سلمنا رسَايلنَا جِريت عالِبيت عَلى طُول.

الجو حَر والسَما صَافْية جِدًا، وتعبني إني مِشيت بسُرعَة تحت شمس حامية كِدَه.

لمَّا وصلت البِيت، أُختِي الكبِيرة قَالِت: **"أهلا يا وليد."**

رِديت: **"أهلا."**

سَألِتني: **"مَالك؟، يُومك كَان وِحِش؟"**

قُلتلهَا: **"كان أسوء يُوم فِي المدرسة."**

"أسعد مجَاش، وكَان فِي ولد عمَّال يضحك علَيا طُول اليُوم."

65

قالِتلي: "دَه مِش حِلْو، تِيجِي نعمِل شَاي وتحكيلي كُل اللي حصل؟"

هزيت راسِي ورُحْت المطبخ عشَان أسخن الميه.

هِيَّ دايمًا بتِعرَف تخِليني أحسَن.

صبِتلي كُبَاية شَاي سُخنة، وأنا أخذَتها وقعدت عَلَى الترابيزة.

سألتِني: "ليه متضايق أوي كِدَه؟"

قُلتلهَا: "بُصِي، كُنت مُتحمِس جِدًا بجد أزُوح المدرسة الصُبح، بس بعد مَا وصلت أخدت بَالِي إني نسِيت إزازة المِيه، أسعد مجَاش وبعدين ولد قعد يضحك عَليا عشَان مِش عارِف أقرأ الكِتاب صَح."

قَالِتلي: "دَه تصَرف قليل الذوق مِنُه، إنتَ شُجَاع جِدًا إنك قرِيت بصُوت عَالِي قُدَّام الفصل كُلُه."

قُلتلها: "وبعدين بدأ يَرْمي حَاجَات عليا، بس أنا كتبت رِسالة لسَارة بعد الغدَا. كُنت حاسِس بالوحِدة، عشَان كِدَه جِيت البِيت عَلَطُول."

قَالِتلي: "حلو، أنا مُتأكِدة إن رِسَالتك هتعجبها!"

"وأسعد مُمكِن يجِي المدرسة بُكرة، وساعِتها إنتَ هتبقَى أحسن مرة تَانية." وأعتقد إن عندهَا حَق.

قُلتِلهَا: **"شُكرًا إنك اتكلمتِي معَايا، أنا بحِبك."**

قَالِت: **"أنا كمَان بحِبك يا وليد"**، وخلَّصِت الشَاي بتاعهَا.

فضِلت أنا عَلى التَرابِيزة أخلَّص الشَاي بِتاعِي، واخواتنَا الخمسَة رِجعُوا البيت مِن مذَارِسهُم.

هُمَّا أصغر مِنَّا عشَان كِدَه بيرُوحُوا مذَارِس تانية.

لمَّا رجعُوا البِيت قعدوا يضحكُوا ويلعبُوا شُوية ألعاب، وحسِيت إنِّي مبسوط إنِّي شُفتُهُم.

مَبعرفش أمسِك نفسِي مِن الضِحك لمَّا يجرُوا ويِجُوا يحضُنُونِي.

بحِسْ بالسعَادة لما يكون حَوليَّا نَاس مبسوطين.

VOCABULARY

مَدرَسة	school	سُخْن	hot
فلوس	money	شَمْس	sun
بيت	house	عَطشان	thirsty
مَوضوع	subject	شُرب	drink
رِياضة	math	إزازَة	bottle
تَلات	Tuesday	شَنطة	bag
صُبح	morning	مِشي	to leave
إتعَلِّم	to learn	غامِض	shady
سَبَب	reason	رِوِش	cool
فِهِم	to understand	جُوَّة	inside
رَقَم	number	زَعلان	upset
مُعادلَة	equation	استَنَّى	to wait
لِوَحدُه	alone	زميل في الفَصل	classmate
وَصَل	to arrive	بِصوت عالي	aloud

Vocabulary

وَحيد	lonely	دور	turn
أحسَن	best	وَلَد	boy
صاحِب	friend	مُشكِلَة	trouble
جِديد	new	إتريَق عَلَى	to make fun of
مُدَرِّس	teacher	وِقِف	to stop
قِرايَة	reading	نِهايَة	end
كِتَاب	book	جُزء	part
غِرِق	to sink	حَس	to feel
دَرس	lesson	فِرِح	to cheer up
قَرَّر	to decide	رَسَم	to draw
رَمَى	to throw	قَذارَة	dirt
خاف	to be afraid	لَزِق	stick
إتعَشَّى	to have lunch	حَضَن	to hug
ساكِت	quiet	شَكل	shape

Vocabulary

وَجبَة	meal	أسلوب	pattern
بَطن	tummy	صورَة	picture
فَصل	classroom	واضِح	clear
صاحِب مِن النِت	penpal	أخت	sister
أمريكا	America	شاي	tea
بَعَت	to send	هز راسه	to nod
جَواب	letter	مَطبَخ	kitchen
إتمَرَّن	to practice	سخَّن	to heat
إنجليزي	English	صَب	to pour
كِتابَة	writing	كُبّايَة	cup
هَوا	air	يِنسي	to forget
صَح	correct	يَعني	mean
شُجاع	brave		

جاوِب بِصَح أو غَلَظ:

أ)   يوسِف وِ عيلْتُه رَاحُوا المَطار بِالليِّل.

ب)   هُمَّ وِصلُوا إيطالْيا بَدْرى الصُبْح.

ت)   يوسِف طَلَب طَبَق مَكَرونَة إسْباجِتّي لنَفسُه.

ث)   في فينيشْيا شَافوا ناس لابسين أَطْقُم سودا وماشكات.

ج)   أم يوسِف وَقَّعِت العَجينَة عَلَى الأرْض.

كَمِّل الجُمَل:

أ)   أبو يوسِف .... العَرَبيّة لـ.......... .

ب)   يوسِف مَعرِفش .... عَشَان مَكانش قادِر ....

ت)   يوسِف .... فينيسيا عَشان كان فيها .... بَدَل ....

ث)   يوسِف إتفَرَّج عَلَى .... وهِي بِتتطِبِخ في .... الكبير.

إخْتار الإجابة الصَّح:

١. العيلّة قَعَدِت أد إيه في إيطاليا؟

أ) شَهر.

ب) أسبوعين.

ت) أسبوع.

٢. لَو يوسِف كان غَني، كان هَيعمِل إيه في الوَقت دَه؟

أ) ياكُل سباجِتي اليوم كُله.

ب) يِنام.

ت) يِلعَب ألعاب فيديو.

٣. إيه نوع الماسك إللي يوسِف إشتَراه؟

أ) ماسك أزرَق بريش.

ب) ماسك إسوِد.

ت) ماسك أحمَر بِريش.

72

NOTES

NOTES

7

نَوَّرت البيت

فتح أحمد عِينيه مِن النُوم بالظبط لمَّا الأتُوبِيس وصل المحطَّة.

وأهُو وصل عَمَّان، عَاصِمة الأُردُن الجَمِيلة.

أحمد دعك عِينيه واتمَطَّع.

رِحلة ساعتين بالأتُوبِيس مِن بلدُه مدِينة الكرك كَانوا حلوين، أحمد نَام فِيهم.

أحمد خَد شنطِته ونزل مِن الأتُوبِيس فِي وسط زحمِة الناس.

كَان فِي نَاس فِي كُل مكَان، وأحمَد مِسِك شنطِتُه كُويس.

شَاف علامة عربية التاكسِي، ومِشى ناحية التاكسِيَّات اللي كانت واقفة طابور وركب أوِّل واحِد.

سأله سواق التاكسِي: **"علَى فِين يا أُستَاذ؟"**

جَاوبه أحمد: **"عَايز أرُوح فُندُق بُرج الأردُن لو سمَحت."**

بدأ التاكسِي يتحرك وِسط زحمِة مدِينة عَمَّان، أحمد كان بيتفَرَّج من الشباك علي الزحمة وكان مِستَغْرَب.

مكنش مُتخَيل إن النَّاس كتِير أوي كِدا، والمُرور زحمَة جِدًا.

في كُل حتَّه حَوَليه كَان سامِع كلكسَات العربيات والأُتُوبِيسَات، ونَاس بتزعق وأطفال بيضحكوا.

المدِينة دِي مُختلفَة جِدًا عن بلدُه.

وبعد رِحلة قُصيَّرة حوالِي خَمَستاشَر دقيقة، وقف التاكسِي قُدام الفُندُق.

أحمد حاسِب السواق وخد شُنطُه لاستقبال الفُندُق.

مُوظف الاستقْبال أكِد له علَى حجزُه وخدُه

لِأوضتُه.

كَانِت أوضَة صُغَيّرة بس نضِيفة.

أحمد حط شَنطِتُه وقعد علَى السرِير، كَان يُوم طويل بالنِسبالُه.

حس إن مُوبايلُه بدأ يتهز ويرِن.

طلعُه مِن جِيبُه ورَدْ: **"ألو!"**

رد صُوت راجِل: **"أهلًا أحمد، أنا أُستَاذ بشِير صَاحِب الشقَّة اللِي إنتَ جَي تشُوفها بُكره."**

أحمد قَال: **"آه تمام!، أهلا أُستَاذ بشِير، أقدر أساعدك إزاي؟"**

أُستَاذ بشِير قال: **"كُنت عَايز أكِد عليك إننا هنتقَابِل قُدام الشقَّة السَاعة حِداشَر الصُبح."**

"تمَام، أشُوفك هِناك في المَعاد إن شَاء الله."

وقفل أحمد المُكالمة.

كَان مُتحمّس إنه هَيِبدأ حياتُه الجدِيدة فِي عَمَّان.

وظيفة جدِيدة، ومدِينة جدِيدة.

بس الأول لازم يجهِّز لنفسُه مكَان يعِيش فِيه.

أحمد صِحى بدرِي تانِي يُوم حاسِس إنه متضَايق وجعَان.

متضَايق عشان زحمة المُرور برّه الفُندقُ كَان صُنوتها غَالِي جِدًا، وجعَان عشَان نَام بدرِي إمبارِح وفاته العشَا.

قام و استحمَّى، وبعدين نزل المطعم فِي صالِة الفُندق.

اختار ترَابِيزة جمب الشِباك وقعد.

جَاله جرسُون وِشه بَشُوش ومعَاه المنيو.

الجرسُون قَال: **"صبَاح الخِير يا فندم، أجيب لحضرِتك قهْوَة تِبدأ بِيها؟"**

أحمد قَالُه: **"أيوة مِن فضلك!"**

لمَّا الجرسُون مِشى، أحمد بصْن علَى المنيو.

كَان عَايز فِطار بسِيط بس يِشَّبِّعْ، فلمَّا رجع الجرسُون مرة تانية بالقهْوَة بتاعتُه، طلب مِنه لبنة بزيت الزَّتُون، وزعتر وعِيش عربِي.

أحمد شِبع علي الأَخِر، وراح عشَان يقَابِل صَاحِب الشقَّة.

كَانِت بس مسافة عِشرين دقيقة مشي مِن الفُندق، وكَان يُوم جمِيل.

الشمس كانِت طالعة، والهُوَا كَان صافِي وحس أحمد بالحيوية.

وهُوَّ ماشي، طلَّع مُوبايلُه واتصل برقم أخُوه عَلِي.

سمرة بِنت عَلِي الصُّغيرة ردت عَلَى التليفُون.

سمرة قَالت: **"عمُّو!"**

أحمد بدأ يحكِيلَها عن كُل حَاجَة فِي رحلتُه لعَمَّان، ويوصفلها المدِينة الكبِيرَة عَاملة إزاي.

كَانِت بتسمعُه، وكُل شوية تقُول: **"الله!"**

تانِي، ده خلى أحمد يبتسم، وهُوَّ بيتْخيِّل عُيون سمرة الواسعة وبُؤَّها وهو مفتوح.

وبعد ما اتكلموا شُوية، سمرة قَالِت لأحمد إن باباها راح السُّوق وسَاب مُوبايلُه فِي البِيت.

أحمد وَعَد سمرة إنه يرجع الشَّهر الجاي عشَان يحضر عِيد مِيلادهَا السَّابِع، وبعدين قَالها معَ السلاَمة.

أحمد بيحِب أولاد وبنَات إخواتُه، وبيتمَنى فِي يُوم مِن الأيَّام يكُون عندُه أطفَال.

مِن مسافة قُريبة كَان قادر يشُوف راجِل قُصير مليَان شُوية وراكِن علَى عربيتُه مِستنِّي قُدام العمارة اللي فِيها الشقَّة.

أحمد قال فِي بالُه: **"أكيد ده الأُستاذ بشِير."**

ولمَّا بصْ على شكْل العمارة عَجَبِتُه جِدًا.

مكنش شكلها قديم بس برضُه مش جدِيد أوي، ودَه بِالظَّبط اللي عَجَب أحمَد.

أُستاذ بشِير قَال وهو بيمد إيده: **"أكيد إنتَ أحمد."**

"أيوة، أهلًا و سهلًا"، وسلّم علِيه بالإيد.

أُستاذ بشِير قَال: **"تمام، تعَالى معَايا. الشقَّة فِي الدور التالِت، فأتمَنى ميكُنش عندك مُشكِلة مع السلالِم."**

مع طلوع السلالِم، أحمد بدأ يحِس بالحَر.

واتمَنى إن الموضوع يِبقَى أحسَن لمَّا الجو يبرد شُوية.

أُستَاذ بشِير خدُه لباب مكتُوب عليه رقم تَلاتَة و تَلاتين وفتحُه.

دخلُوا جوّه الشقَّة، والصالة كانت مِنورة.

كَان فِي مطبخ صُغير علَى اليمِين، بس مُجهَّز تجهيز كُويس وبلكُونة روعة بتطُل علَى الشارِع اللِي تحت.

الأُستَاذ بشِير قَال: **"الشقَّة دِي مِثالية فعلًا لِلي إنتَ محتاجُه يا أحمد. هيَّ فِي موقِع مُمتَاز، وفي وسط البلد وفِي حدُود ميزانيتك."**

أحمد اتفق مع رأي المَالِك، وفِضِل يتمشى جوّه الشقَّة.

كَانِتْ حلوة، ومش صُغيرة أوي.

كَان حاسس إنَّها مريحة.

أحمد قَال: **"هاخُدها."**

"مُمتَاز، سعر الإيجَار تُلتُمِيّة وخَمَستَاشَر دِينار في الشَّهر، زي ما قُلتلك قبل كِده. وتكلِفة الفَواتير حوالِي خَمسين دِينار في الشَّهر."

أحمد قَال: **"تمام، مفيش مُشكلة"**، وكان بيحسب الإجمالِي فِي دماغُه بسُرعة: (تُلتُمِيّة

خَمسَة وسِتّين دِينار).

"تمام جِدًّا، أنا سعِيد إنّي أجرتلك الشقَّة دِي."

"تقدر تِنقل فِيها مِن بُكرَه، هقابلك هِنا السَاعة تِسعَة الصُبح وأديك المفَاتِيح."

"استنى أجِبلك عقد الإيجَار مِن شنطِتي."

ولمَّا كَان أُستَاذ بشِير بيدور فِي شنطِتُه، أحمد طلع البلكونة.

وكَان قادر يشم رِيحة المدِينة، روَايح كتِير مُختلفة كَانِتْ حَوَليه.

كَان فِي حيَاة كاملة حَوَليه، وحِسّ بامتنان كبِير إنه جَتلُه الفُرصَة يعيش فِي عَمَّان.

الموضوع هَيِبقى مُغامرة جدِيدة بالنسبالُه.

بعد توقيع عقد الإيجار أُستَاذ بشِير نِزِل مع أحمد مِن الشقَّة علَى السلمِ قبل ما يقوله مع السلامة.

وبما إنه فاضِي بعد الضُهر وقُريِّب مِن فندقه، فكر أحمد إنه يستكشِف حي سكنُه الجدِيد.

لمَّا خد شارِع شِمال بعد العمارة اللي فيها شقتُه، لقَى نفسُه فِي شارِع مُحاط مِن

الناحيتين بشجر، وفِيه محلات صغيرة كتِير وكافِيهات.

وهُوَّ بيتمشَّى لأخِر الشارِع، وقف قُدام محل عصير عَندُه قعدة صُغيرة برَّه.

خدلُه كُرسِي، وفجأة لقَى نفسُه عطشَان جِدًا.

فِي الكرك، محل العصير اللِي فِي قريته كَان معروف إنه أحسن محل عصير فِي المدِينة.

أحمد فكر: **"خلِّينَا نشُوف بتاع عَمَّان أخباره إيه"**

الشمس كانت فوق رَاسُه. طلب عصِير بُرتقَان، وخدْ أول شفطة.

ولأول مرة مِن ساعِة ما وصل، أحمد حس بالراحَة والسعَادة.

لقَى أحمد كُورة بتتدحرج لحد رجله ولمَّا بص، شَاف مجموعة مِن الأولاد واقفِين فِي دايرة.

أحمد خد الكُورة، ورمَاها تانِي للمجموعة.

واحد مِن الأولاد مسك الكُورة وقَال: **"شكرا!"**

الولد سأله: **"إنتَ ساكِن هِنَا يا أُستَاذ؟"**

أحمد فكَّر شوية في السؤال.

وبعد كِده رد بابتسامة، وقال: **"أيوة، أنا سَاكِن هِنَا."**

VOCABULARY

أَجَّر	to rent	نِزِل	to climb down
شِقَّة	apartment	مِشي عَند	to step into
فَتَح	to open	زَحمَة	crowd
باص	bus	قَفَل كوِّيس	to tighten
مَحَطَّة	station	مِيسِك	grip
عاصِمَة	capital	لاحِظ	to spot
دَعَك	to rub	تاكسي	taxi
مَط	to stretch	سوَّاق	driver
كِتاف	arms	مَشغول	busy
مَسقَط رأس	home town	مَدينَة	city
مُمتِع	pleasant	دَهشَة	amazement
مِيسِك	to pick up	يِسمَع	to hear
شَنطِة سَفَر	suitcase	بوق	horn
زَعَّق	to shout	صوت	voice

85

Vocabulary

مُختَلِف	different	أكّد	to confirm
شُنَط سَفَر	luggage	قابِل	to meet
ظُرفَة	lobby	عَلَّق	to hang up
موظَّف الاستِقبال	receptionist	كان مُتَشَوِّق	to be excited
حَجز	reservation	حياة	life
إهتَز	to vibrate	شُغل	job
رَّن	to ring	رَتِّب	to organize
مالِك	landlord	صِحي	to wake up
مُتَوَتِّر	irritated	سوق	market
مرور	traffic	وَعَد	to promise
إستَحَمَّى	to shower	رِجع	to return
إختار	to choose	قُصيِّر	short
قَعَد	to sit	مِدوَّر	round
مُرضي	satisfying	إندَّهش	to be impressed

VOCABULARY

بَسيط	simple	تابِع	to follow
زَعتَر	zaatar	سلاليم	stairs
لبنة	labneh	أرض	floor
عيش	flatbread	حَرارَة	heat
لَمَع	to shine	جَّو	weather
عايِش	alive	مِتجَهِّز	well-equipped
جيب	pocket	كوَّيِس	
		جذَّاب	charming
إتصَل	to dial	بَلَكونة	balcony
زَعَّق	to shout	مَكان	location
بُق	mouth	مَركَزي	central
نبذَة	brief	ميزانيّة	budget
شَرَح	to explain	فَتِّش	to rummage
خَدَمات	utilities	نَكهَة	aroma
حَسَب	to calculate	طَفَى	to float

87

Vocabulary

المَجموع الكُلّي	total sum	وَقَّع	to sign
دينار	dinar	بَعد الضُّهر	afternoon
مُفتاح	key	إستَكشِف	to explore
عَقد إيجار	lease	مِخضِرّة	leafy
شَنطة	briefcase	مَحَّل	store
إتجوّل	to wander	مِرتاح	relaxed
فَجأة	suddenly	عاش	to live
فَكَّر	to think	ظَلَب	to order

جاوِب بِصَح أو غَلَظ:

أ)   رَقَم شَقَّة أحْمَد الجديدَّة خَمْسين.

ب)   أحْمَد كَلْ زَعتَر عَلَى الفِطار.

ت)   المَطبَخ في الناحْية الشِمال مِن بيتُه الجِديد.

ث)   الشَقَّة الجِديدَة مَفيهاش بَلَكونَة.

ج)   سميرَة عَنذَها سَبَع سِنين.

كَمِّل الجُمَل:

أ)   أحْمَد مِن ....

ب)   بَعد ما وِصيل، .... قَعَد في أوتيل .... في عَمَّان.

ت)   الشَقَّة عَلَى مسافِة .... مَشي مِن الفُندُق.

ث)   أحْمَد قَعَد في بار .... عَشان كان ....

89

إخْتار الإجابة الصَّح:

١. تاكسي أحْمَد وِقِف فين؟

أ) في المُنتَزَه.

ب) قُدَّام الفُندُق.

ت) قُدَّام مَبنَى الشقَّة.

٢. أحْمَد كان متضَايق ليه؟

أ) كان تَعبان من كُتر السَفَر.

ب) صوت العَرَبيَّات بَرَّة كان عالي أوي.

ت) مكانش فيه قَهوَة.

٣. أحْمَد هيدفَع كام لشَقَّتُه؟

أ) خَمسين دينار في الشَهر.

ب) رُبعوميَة خَمسَة وسِتين دينار في الشَهر.

ت) تُلتوميَة خَمسَة وسِتين دينار في الشَهر.

NOTES

NOTES

8

هَدَف

وليد بينادي مِن الجمب التاني للملعب: **"باصي الكُورة يا محمد!"**

ومحمد كَان قُريّب جِدًا مِن الجُون و كَان غارِف إنّه هَيقدَر يِجيب جُون.

جرى بالكُورة قُدامُه وبأقصى تركيز، محمد كَان سامِع ضربَات قلبُه بصُوت عالِي فِي وِدنُه.

طنّش زمايله الي بيندهوا عليه، وشَاط الكُورة بكُل ما عنده مِن قُوة.

جُووون!؛ صُوت عالِي مِن الجمبين في الملعب، وحس محمد بزيادة الأدرينالين فِي جسمه.

وزمايله فِي الفِريق اتجمعُوا حَوَليه، وهتفُوله ورفعُوه فِي الهَوَا.

محمد فِرح جِدًا.

فِريقه كسب بسبَبُه.

وفِي غرف تغيير الملابِس زمايل محمد فِضلُوا يطبطبوا على كِتفُه ويهنُّوه.

بَاب غُرفِة تغيير الملابِس اتفتح ودخل مِنه مُدرب الفِريق، كابِتن شِفِيق.

كابِتن شِفِيق قَال وهو بيسلم على محمد بالإيد: **"برافو عليك النهارده يا محمد، كُنت هَايِل."**

"فِي الواقِع، مُمتَاز لدرجِة إن النَّادي عَايز يبعَتك فِي مِنحة لكُورة القدم تزُوح تِلعب فِي إنجلترا السنة الجاية."

كُل الفِريق سِكت، ومحمد فتح بُؤه.

محمد سَأل: **"إيه؟، أنا أرُوح أعيش فِي إنجلترا؟"**

المُدرِّب قَال: **"أيوة، وطبعًا هَيكُون لازم تاخُد دُروس فِي الإنجليزي طُول الفترة اللي فاضلة مِن السنة دي فِي مدرسَة مُتخصّصة، بس دَه مِش هِيكُون مُشكِلة بالنسبالك."**

بيب بيب! وصوت المنبه بيطفي.

النَهارده أول حصة ليه فِي مدرِسة اللغة المُتخصّصة.

محمد كَان بيتكلّم شُوية إنجليزي، بس مكنش حتى قُرِيّب مِن إنه يبقَى جَاهِز يعيش فِي دولة بتتكلّم إنجليزي.

مشوَار الأتُوبِيس لمدرِسة اللغة حوالي عِشرِين دقيقة مِن شقتُه.

وقف الأتُوبِيس قُدام مبنى أحمر كِبِير جِدًا.

وكَان فِيه طُلاب فِي كل مكَان بيتحركُوا بسُرعة.

كمل محمد طريقُه لمكتب الاستِقبَال.

وكَان فِي سِت لَطِيفة شقرة قاعدة على مكتب الاستِقبَال.

سأِلت وهي بتتكلم إنجليزي بسرُعَة: **"أهلاً، أقدر أساعدك إزاي؟"**

رد محمد ببُطء: **"أهلاً... إسمِي محمد ..."**

حسّت السِت إن دَه طَالِب جِدِيد، وابتسِمت بلُطف وغيّرِت سُرعة كلامهَا.

"أهلًا يا محمد، إسمِي ليزا وأهلًا بيك فِي مدرسة عَمَّان المُتخصّصة فِي اللغة."

"اسمحِلي أوريك فصلك."

فِهم تقْرِيبًا نُص اللِي قَالِته ليزا بس، وهز راسُه ومشى وراهَا فِي ممر طوِيل.

وصلِتُه لفصل فِيه اتناشَر طالِب قاعدين على دِسكات.

"روزا، ده محمد. طالِب جِدِيد، أُردِني الجنسِية."

روزا، سِت كِبيرة لِيها ابتسَامة عرِيضة.

روزا قَالِت وهِيّ بتشَاور على الدسكات: **"أهلًا يا محمد، أهلًا بيك فِي الفصل."**

"لو سمحت اقْعُد على واحد مِن الدسكات."

محمد شكَر ليزا ومشى للدّسك اللي جمب الحيطة.

نزّل شنطِتُه وقعد على الكُرسِي.

وبص حولِيه، وشاف محمد أن كُل الطُلاب التانِيين شكلُهم عرب برضه.

بص على الدسك اللِّي جمبه، كان قاعِد عليه شاب.

96

ابتسم فِي وشه ومَدِلُه إيده.

الشاب قَال بالعربي: **"أهلًا، أنا عُمران."**

محمد رد: **"أهلًا، أنا محمد، اتشرفت بمعرِفتك."**

"مع إنِّي شِبه مُتأكِّد إن إحنَا المفرُوض نتكلَّم إنجليزي."

ضِحك عُمران، **"أيوة مُمكِن، بس أحيانًا بيكون أسهل بكتِير إننا نتكلَّم بلغُتنَا الأصلية!"**

وبعد سَاعة مِن الجِصة، حس محمد بإن تركِيزُه قَل.

كَان الموضُوع صعب جِدًا.

كُل حَاجَة كَانِت بالإنجليزي!.

لو حبُّوا يسألُوا سُؤال لازم يسألُوه بالإنجليزي.

وكُل حَاجَة بتقُولهَا روزا بتكُون بالإنجليزي.

محمد كَان مِحتَاج يرُوح الحَمَّام.

(إيه الفرق بين "فين" و"مين" ؟). محمد رفع إيده.

روزا قَالِت: **"نعم يا محمد؟"**

سَألها محمد بالإنجليزي: **"همممم، مين الحَمَّام؟"**

انفجِرِت مُوجة ضِحك خَفِيفة فِي الفَصل واحمَرْ وِش محمد.

بص بسرعة لصاحبْه الجدِيد، اللِي بص لمحمد بابتسَامِة تعاطُف.

روزا قَالِت وهِيَّ بتشاور لناحية الشِمال: **"أعتقد قصدك "فين" يا محمد، مِش "مين"، بس مُحاولة كُويسة!"**

"الحمَّامَات برَّه الفصُول فِي نهاية القَاعة."

لمَّا محمد رِجع، كَان لازِم يكوِّنُوا مجموعات من اتنين ويكمِّلُوا تمرِين: يِعَرَّفوا نفسُهُم.

محمد كان مع عُمران فِي المجموعة، ودِي حَاجَة بسطته.

عُمران قَال بالعربِي: **"طيب، هبدأ أنا."**

عمرِان قال بالإنجليزي ببطء بس بلغة سليمة: **"أهلًا، اسمِي عُمرِان، عندِي سِتة وعِشْرِين سنة وأنا طالِب فِي جامعة عَمَّان."**

"بدرِس هندسة، أعزب وبحب كُورة القدم."

محمد قال بالعربي: **"إيه ده!، إنتَ مُمتَاز. بقَالك قد إيه بِتتعلِّم؟"**

روزا سِمعتهم وجتلهُم.

"ياشباب لو سمحتُم التزموا بالإنجليزي."

"أنا عَارفة إنه الموضُوع صعب، بس فِي مدرسِة اللغة الإنجليزي هِيَّ اللغة الوحيدة اللِي بنتكلِّم بيها جُوَّه الفصُول عشَان تساعدكم تِتعلِّموا أسرع."

الاتنين قالوا: **"أسِفين."**

"ماشي. إسمِي محمد، وأنا ... تمانية وعشرين سنة ... "

عُمران قَالُه: **"عندِي."**

"أيوة عندى. بلعب كُورة قدم ... النَّادِي بتَاعي هِيبعتني لإنجلترا ... فِي مِنحة."

عُمران قَال: **"بجد؟ ده شِيء رائِع!"**

محمد سأله: **"رائِع؟"**

"أيوة، رائِع كلمة بنقُولهَا لمَّا الحاجة تبقى عظِيمة."

محمد قَال: **"آه تمام."** هو كَان سِمع الكِلمة دي كذَا مرة فِي أفلام أمرِيكِية.

بعد كِدَه فِي الليلة دِي محمد كَان مُرهق ومِمدد على السرِير.

قَال لنفسِه: **"تعلُّم لغة تانية أكيد خلاك مُرهق."**

وقرر يتفرج على فِيلم أمرِيكِي على نيتفليكس بترجمة إنجليزي على الشَّاشة.

إختار فِيلم **"الفطيرة الأمرِيكية"**، وضغط عرض.

فِي نُص الفِيلم حس محمد إن دِماغُه شوشِت.

فكَان لازم يوقف؛ عشَان كِدَه بقت معلُومَات زيادة على مُخُه.

كَان مِن الصعب قِراية الترجمة اللي مكتُوبة على الشَّاشة، والتركِيز مَع الكلام اللِي بيتقَال بالإنجليزي.

ورغم كِدَه إتعاهد محمد قدام نفسُه إنُّه يتفَرَّج على فِيلم كُل ليلة بترجمة إنجليزي على الشَّاشة لحد مَا يتقن اللغة.

عدى شهر، ومحمد كَان بيحضر فِي مدرِسة

اللغة كُل يُوم لمُدة تَلَاتْ سَاعَات.

واتفاجئ بالفعل بالكمِّية اللي اتعلِّمها خِلال الفترة القُصيرة دِي.

روزا سَألِت: **"ماشي يا جماعة، مُستعدِّين النَهارده نِعمِل عرض حوارات قصيرة؟"**

"محمد، ابتدي إنت الأول."

قام محمد ومشى لأول الفصل.

كَان مُستعد لِكِدَه، وكَان بيتمرن طُول الأُسبُوع اللي فَات وحفظ العرض.

"أهلًا، أنا محمد، عندِي تمانية وعشرين سنة وبشتغل فِي مطعم."

"بحب ألعب كُورة والنَّادِي بتَاعِي هِيبعتِني لإنجلترا فِي مِنحة السَنة الجَاية."

"عُمري ما رُحت إنجلترا، بس أعتقد إنها هتعجبِني."

"عندِي أخ واحد أكبر مِني، وأُخت واحدة أصغر مِني."

"أنا ساكِن على بُعد عِشرين دقيقة مِن مدرِسة اللغة دِي."

"أكلِتي المُفضَّلة هِيَّ الطعميّة، ومشرُوبِى المُفضّل هُوَّ القِهْوَة."

"وعَايز أتعلّم إنجليزي عشَان أقدر أعمِل صداقَات فِي إنجلترا.

"ومُممكِن حتى ألاقِي زوجة هِنَاك."

الفصل كله بِمَا فِيهُم روزا ضِحكُوا.

"برافو يا محمد!، ده كَان أداء مُمتَاز. طيب، دلوقتِي فِي أي حد عندُه أي أسئِلة لمحمد؟"

واحدة قاعدة فِي الصف اللِي قُدام رفعِت إيدها وسألت: **"إيه مَوقِعك فِي ملعب كُورة القدم يا محمد؟"**

محمد عَارف الإجابة. **"أنا لاعِب خط وِسط شمال، بس أحب إني أكُون حارِس مرمى برضه."**

روزا قَالِت: **"عظيم، أي أسئلة تانية؟"**

راجل قاعد وزَا رفع إيده وسأل: **"هتفضَّل قد إيه فِي إنجلترا؟"**

"سَنَة وَاحدَة."

روزا قَالِت: "تمَام، سُؤال واحد كمَان."

وقَال عُمران: "إيه أحسن حَاجَة عملتَها السنَة دِي يا محمد؟"

اِبتَسَم محمد وقال: "اتعلّمت أتكلّم إنجليزي."

Vocabulary

تَغطِيَة	immersion	زَميل في الفَريق	teammate
زَعَّق	to yell	شاط	to kick
جَمب	side	هَدَف	goal
ميدان	field	صَرخَة	roar
قَفل	close	خَط جانبي	sideline
هَدَف	goal	ينفَجِر	to erupt
وِدان	ears	أديرنالين	adrenaline
كِيسب	to beat	إندَفَع	to surge
قَلب	heart	جِسم	body
تِركيز	concentration	إتجَمَّع	to rally
نَطَّط الكورَة	to dribble	شال	to lift
تجاهل	to ignore	كِيسب	to win
مُكالمَة	call (noun)	تغيير الأوضَة	change room
فَريق	team	نادي	club

Vocabulary

ظَبظَب	to pat	مِنحَة دِراسيّة	scholarship
ضَهر	back	إنجلترا	England
قال مَبروك	to congratulate	سكوت	silent
أوضية اللبس	locker room	مُشكِلَة	problem
مُدرّب	coach	مِنَبّه	alarm
تُحفَة	fantastic	لُغَة	language
هَز	to shake	مِبنَى	building
ريسيبشَن	reception	كوريدور	corridor
أشقَر	blonde	أردُني	Jordanian
شَعر	hair	حَدَّد	to point
سَريع	fast	عَرَب	Arab
بِبُطئ	slowly	اللُغَة الأم	native language
عَدّل	to adjust	دَرس	lesson
سُرعَة	speed	فَصل	class

Vocabulary

هَز راسُه	to nod	صَعب	difficult
إنجليزي	English	شِمال	left
حَمَّام	bathroom	قَدّم	to introduce
رَفَع	to raise	شارِك	to be partnered
حَمَّام	toilet	هَندَسة	engineering
نُص ضيحكة	snicker	كورَة	soccer
أحمَر	red	حِلو	awesome
وِدّي	sympathetic	عَناوين فَرعيّة	subtitles
ضَغَط	to press	حمولَة زايدَة	overload
لِعب	play	وَعَد	to vow
عَقل	brain	بَقى خَبير	to master
ضَبابي	foggy	حَضَر	to attend
مَعلومات	information	مُحادَثة	dialogue
إتمَرَّن	to practise	عَرض	presentation

Vocabulary

زوجَة	*wife*	مُمتاز	*excellent*
سؤال	*question*	مَوقِع	*position*

جاوِب بِصَح أو غَلَظ:

أ)   مُدَرِّب مِحَمَّد اسمُه وَليد.

ب)   مَدرَسِة اللُغات بَعْد نُص ساعَة مِن بيتُه.

ت)   مِحَمَّد بيتْكَلِّم إنْجِليزي حِلو أوي.

ث)   الحَمَّامات في آخِر الطُرقَة.

ج)   مِحَمَّد إتفَرَّج عَلَى فيلْم إنْجِليزي بِتَرجَمَة عَرَبي.

كَمِّل الجُمَل:

أ)   مِحَمَّد هَيروح .... عَشَان مِنحَة ....

ب)   .... الفَصل .... إنْجِليزي بَس.

ت)   مِحَمَّد .... إنّه .... عَلَى فيلم كُل ليلَة.

ث)   مِحَّمد عَندُه .... وعِشرين سَنَة و .... في مَطعَم.

إِخْتار الإِجابة الصَّح:

١. إيه لون مَبنَى مَدرَسة اللُغات؟

أ) أزرَق.

ب) أحمَر.

ت) أبيَض.

٢. إيه لون شَعر ليزا؟

أ) بُنِّي.

ب) إسوِد.

ت) أشقَر.

٣. مِحَمَّد هيعيش في إنجِلِترا أد إيه؟

أ) سِت شُهور.

ب) سَنَتين.

ت) سَنَة.

Notes

NOTES

9

ياه، يا دُكتور

كَان الجَو دافِي، والنُور بيلمع على وِش النهر.

الكلاَم كَان مُستمِر، الأكل والمشْروبَات كَانِت لِذيذة والشِيشَة كَانِت أحسن وأحسن.

عُمَر بص حوليه على مجموعة صُحَاب قاعِدِين كُلُّهُم فِي دايرة، وبيقضُّوا ليلة جمِيلة.

سَألُه أعز أصحَابه إبراهِيم: **"بس بجد ياعُمَر، تفتكر إنت هِتتجوز إمتَى؟"**

عُمَر كَرمِش مندِيل ورمَاه على وشُّه.

و رَدْ عُمَر: **"مِش قُريب خَالِص، أنا شَاب صُغير. مكملتش حتى تمانيَة وعِشرين سنة.   عَايز**

أتأكَّد إنِّي أتجوِّز الزُوجة المِناسبة ومعتقدْش إنِّي قابِلتهَا لحد دلوقتِي."

ضِحكُوا أصحَابُه وهزُّوا روسهُم.

فَهِمُوا الوضع.

فِي الحقِيقة، كَان فِي راجِل واحِد بس مِن المجمُوعة دِي هُوَّ اللِي مِتجوِّز.

كَان قابِل مِراتُه فِي سن صُغير جِدًا؛ فِي سن التِسَعتاشَر.

وصل الجرسُون بشِيشَة جدِيدة وفحم سُخن.

عُمَر كَان عارِف إنه مِش صحِّي بالنسبالُه، بس كَان بيِجِب يشرب شِيشَة حلوة مِن وقت للتاني.

عُمَر اِحتاج يرُوح الحمَّام، فوقف ومشى جُوَه المطعم.

وفجأة بَاب اتفَتح بسُرعة مِن الجنب الشّمال للقاعة وخبط عُمَر جَامِد.

عُمَر قَال: "oIIIآ"، ووقع لوزَا.

قَالِت البِنت: "أنا أسفة جِدًا.. مكنش قصدِي.. بَاب الحمَّام الغبِي ده كَان معصلج فاضطرِيت أزقُّه جَامِد."

114

بص عُمَر للبِنت، ولثواني حس إن قلبِه وقف.

كَانِت جمِيلة جِدًا.

عيُونها الخضَرا كَانِت واسعة وصادقة، وهي بتمد إيدها تقَوِّم عُمَر.

عُمَر مسك إيدها ورفع نفسُه.

وقَال: **"مفِيش مُشكِلة. حصل خير، بتحصل الحَاجَات دِي."**

البِنت قَالِت: **"مُتأكِّد إنك كُويِس؟ مُحرجة جِدًا إنِّي وقعت راجِل زيك على الأرض."**

"أيوِة أيوة، أنا كويِّس. أهلًا، أنا عُمَر. واتشَرفت... بمعرِفتك!"

ضِحِكِت البِنت، وعُمَر لاحظ إنَّها مَكْسُوفة ووشها أحْمَر.

"أهلًا يا عُمَر، أنا نُورا. ومرة تانية، أنا أسفة على اللي حصَل. أتمِنى بقِية ليلتك تبقَى سعِيدة."

وبعْد الكلمِتين دُول، لِفِت ومشيت.

عُمَر دخل الحمَّام و شَاف نفسُه فِي المراية. كَان شكلُه أهبل، وقَال فِي بالُه: **"إيه البِنت الجمِيلة دِي."**

عُمَر صِحِى الصبح تاني يُوم علَى وَجَع صعب جِدًا فِي زوزُه.

حس بزوزُه ملتهب، زي ما يكون حد عمَّال يخربش فِيه كُل مرة يبلع فِيهَا ريقُه.

عُمَر مكنش كويِّس، وقَال فِي بَالُه، شكلِي كِدَه شِربِت شِيشَة كتِير ليلة إمبارح.

قَام مِن السرِير، وراح الحمَّام، وفتح بُؤُه جامد وبص فِي المراية.

"أوووه" قَال فِي بَاله: **"شكلُه كِدَه مش تمام."** كَان زوزُه مُلتِهب و مِحمِرْ جامِد. **"أكيد ده محصلِش بسبب شُرب الشِيشَة بس."**

اتنهَّد عُمَر وخد موبايلُه عشَان يحجز معاد مع دُكتورُه.

"ألو يا دُكتور، مع حضرِتك عُمَر سيد. مِحتاج أجِي أزور حضرِتك، زُوري مُلتِهب جِدًا وعَايزك تُبَص علِيه."

"أيوة يا عُمَر. طيب، تقدر تيجِي النَهَارده، بس أنا همشِي بدري النهَارده، ففِي دُكتور تانِي هِيكشِف عليك بدالِي."

"تمام يا دُكتور، أقدر أجِي بعد الضُهر؟"

"أيوة، هحجزلك مَعاد. مع السلامَة يا عُمَر."

عُمَر قعد يقلّب فِي مجلة قدِيمة فِي غُرفِة الانتِظار. وسأل نفسُه: **"ليه فِي غُرف انتِظار الدكاترة كُل المجَلات قدِيمة؟"**

نادى صُوت نِسائي: **"عُمَر سيد؟"**

رجَّع عُمَر المجلة مرة تانية على التَرابيزة، وقَام وقف.

وقفت قُدامُه، بتنادِي على اسمُه ... البِنت بتاعِت ليلة امبارح، نُورا.

قَالِت وهيَّ ماشية قدامه لمكتبهَا: **"تعَالى معَايا لو سمحت يا عُمَر."**

راح وراها على مكتبهَا وقعد على كُرسِي المريض، ونُورا قعدِت على مكتبهَا.

"نُورا؟ مِش معقُول، إيه المُفاجأَة دي. إنتي دُكتورة؟"

نُورا قالِت: **"أيوة، الدُنيا صُغيرة أوي. أتمنى متكُنش جيْ النهَاردة بِسبب وقعِة ليلة امبارح؟"**

"لا..لا.. أنا هِنا عشَان ... " اتردد عُمَر واتكَسِفْ

117

وحس إنه عبيط.

البِنت عجبِتُه. وهُوَّ هَيُقعُد ويفتحلهَا بُؤه فِعلًا عشَان تِبُص فِيه؟

"أيوة؟ كمِّل يا عُمَر."

عُمَر قَال: **"آه، أنا صحِيت النهَارده الصُّبح عَلَى حرقَان فِي زوزُي و شكلُه مُلتهِب جِدًا."**

"طِيب، فِي أي أعرَاض تانية؟؛ صُدَاع؟، احتقَان فِي الأنف؟ أو سُخونية؟"

"لا، بس مش حاسِس إني مظبُوط. مُمكِن سُخن شُوية."

نُورا خِدِت خافِض اللسان ولفت حولين المكتب مِن الجمب التانِي.

"افتح بُؤَّك لو سمحت وقُول (oIIآ)."

عُمَر رجع راسُه لِوَرا وفتح بُؤه. وكان مكسوف.

نُورا ضغطت بخافِض اللسان على لسَانُه و بصِّت.

"هممممم، صح. اللُوز بتاعتك مُلتهِبة جِدًا. شَايفَاها حَالِة التهَاب لُوز عَامَة. هتِحتَاج تاخُد مُضَادات حيَوية عشَان تِخف مِنهَا."

118

عُمَر قَال: "تمام، شُكرًا إنك كشفتِي عليا."

"أَكِيد!. أنا دُكتورة، دَه شُغلِي."

عُمَر حس إن وِشه اِحمَرْ.

"وكمَان هِتحتَاج تتمَضمَض وِتِتغرغَر بميه بملح، عشَان تقلِّل الألم والوَرَم."

نُورا قَالِت: "خليني أبُص على وِدانك كِدَه كمَان"، وهِيَّ بتوجه كشَاف جُوَاهُم.

"تمام..شايفاهم كُوِيسِين. خليني أقيس درجِة حرارتك."

نُورا أخدِت تِرمُومِتر مِن مكتبَها، وطلبت مِن عُمَر يُحطُّه تحت باطه.

سَألها عمر: "بقالِك كَام سنة دُكتورة؟"

"دِي السنة التالتة ليا كدُكتورة مُمَارسة. اتخرَّجت وأنا صُغيرة شُوية."

سَألها عُمَر: "مُمكِن أسألِك عندِك كَام سنة؟، ولا تِبقَى وقَاحة مِنِّي؟"

ضحكت نُورا وردَّت: "عندِي تِسعَة وعِشرين سنة."

عُمَر قَال: "يااه! أكبر مِني بسنتِين بس." وقَال

119

فِي بَالُه: "امسِك فِي الفرصة."

البنت جمِيلة، وذكِية. ومكِنِتش صدُفة إنك تِخبط فِيها ليلة امبارح فِي المطعم و كمان النهَاردة.

"مممم، دُكتورة نُورا، أنا عَارِف إن ده مُمكِن يُكُون مِش مُنَاسِب خَالِص، بس كُنت عَايز أسألِك لو كُنتِي تحبِي نِتقَابِل نِشرب قَهْوَة مَع بعض لمَّا أخِفْ؟. أنا عَارِف إنِّي معرفكِيش خَالِص، بس مَقْدِرتش أمنع نفسِي مِن إنِّي ألاحِظ قد إيه إنتِي جمِيلة لمَّا، إحم، خبطِيني ليلة إمبارح بالبَاب بالغلط. وبايِن عليكِي إنك إنسَانة لطِيفة، فأتمنىَ بجد إني أتعرف عليكِي أكتر. لو توافقِي."

عُمَر لاحِظ إنُه كَان بِيرغِي وإنْ التِرمُومِتر لِسَه تحت بَاطُه.

وبدأ يصفَّر، فشالُه مِن تحت بَاطُه.

ابتسمت نُورا: **"حرارة جِسمك مُرتِفِعة شُوية، بس ده عشَان جِسمك فِيه عدوى. وأيوة يا عُمَر. أحِب أشرب قَهْوَة معَاك، دلوقتِي رُوح واستِرَيَّح."**

120

شكرهَا عُمَر وهِيَّ بتدِيلُه الرُّوشِتة وخرج مِن المكتب.

كَان بيكره إنه يعيى، بس المرة دِي قَال فِي بَاله:
"حظ سعِيد وكرم."

راح لمكتب الاستِقْبال ودفع تَلاتين دِينار فلُوس الكشف.   ولِحُسن الحظ كَانِت فِي صيدلية جمبُه، فسلَّم الرُّوشِتة واستنَى.

الصَيدلِي كَان راجِل كبِير في السن ..   و ندَه:
"عُمَر سيد؟"

"أيوة"، وراحلُه عُمَر.

"طيب، لازم تأخُد المُضَادَات الحيَوية دِي مرتين فِي اليُوم بعد الأكل لمُدة أسبُوع.   لو محسِّتش بتحسُن ساعِتها، لازم تِرجع للدُكتور تانِي ...   "، وبص الصيدِلي فِي الرُّوشِتة.

"آه، نُورا.. سِت جمِيلة جِدًا، مِش كده؟"

ابتسم عُمَر: **"أيوة جمِيلة."**

VOCABULARY

دُكتور	doctor	أنوار	lights
هَوا	air	نَهر	river
دافي	warm	لَمَع	to shine
مُحادثّة	conversation	أكل	food
شيشة	shisha	صُحاب	friends
إتجَوّز	to get married	طَلَّع صوت عالي	to scrunch
مَنديل	napkin	رَمى	to throw
إتأكّد	to make sure	قابِل	to meet
فَحم	coal	صَحّي	healthy
دَخّن	to smoke	شِرِب سَجاير	to need
وِقِف	to stand up	ضَرَب	to hit
وِقِع	to fall	إتأسّف	to be sorry
حادثّة	accident	غَبي	stupid
زَق	to push	قَلب	heart

122

VOCABULARY

جِميل	beautiful	مُخلِص	sincere
حَصَل	to happen	تَفوَّق	to knock down
أرض	ground	وِشُه إحمَّر	to blush
مِرايَة	mirror	جَبان	sheepish
جَميل	gorgeous	رَهيب	terrible
حَنجَرة	throat	خام	raw
قَشَّر	to scrape	ضوافِر الصوابِع	fingernails
بلَع	to swallow	إلتَهَب	to be inflamed
يِحَدِّد مَعاد	to make an appointment	إلتهاب	sore
مَجَلَّة	magazine	صوت	voice
مَريض	patient	مَكسوف	shy
صُداع	headache	زُكام	nasal congestion
حَرارة	fever	يمَيِّل	to tilt
سَخيف	silly	لِسان	tongue

Vocabulary

إلتهاب اللِوَز	tonsillitis	لِوَز	tonsils
يشَطِّف	to rinse	مُضادَّات حَيَويّة	antibiotics
ميّا مالحَة	salt water	إتغَرغَر	to gargle
عَرَق	swelling	وَجَع	pain
تِرمومِتر	thermometer	دَرَجة حَرارَة	temperature
إتخَرَّج	to graduate	بَطاط	armpit
روشِتّة	prescription	وَقِح	rude

جاوِب بِصَح أو غَلَظ:

أ) عُمَر عَنْدُه تَمانْيَة وعِشْرين سَنَة.

ب) عُمَر رَمَى مَنْديل عَلَى صاحْبُه.

ت) عُمَر إحْتاج دُكْتور عَشان وَجَع بَطْنُه.

ث) نورا أصْغَر مِن عُمَر.

ج) عُمَر دَفَع تَلاتين دولار عَشان يِروح لِلدُكْتور.

كَمِّل الجُمَل:

أ) عُمَر .... عالْيَة عَشان عَنْدُه عَدْوَى.

ب) .... جَمْب مَكْتَب الدُكْتور.

ت) عُمَر عَنْدُه .... حَمْرا و ....

ث) عُمَر مَعَنْدوش .... وَلا زُكّام.

إخْتار الإجابة الصَّح:

١. صُحاب عُمَر كانوا قاعدين إزّاي؟

أ) إتنين إتنين.

ب) عَند ظرابيزَة مُربَّعة.

ت) في دايرَة.

٢. عُمَر حَس إنه تَعبان عَشان

أ) شِرِب شيشا كِتير.

ب) شِرِب كِتير.

ت) كانِت عَندُه اللوَز.

٣. عُمَر عَزَم نورا عَلَى

أ) رَقص.

ب) تِشرَب شيشا.

ت) تِشرَب قَهوَة.

NOTES

NOTES

10

فُرصَة دَهبيَّة

راندا بِتشتَغل فِي شِركة بنكية بقَالها خمس
سِنِين، وكَانت مُوظفة درجة أولى.

كَانت دايمًا بتِيجِي فِي معَادها، وتشتَغل عدد
ساعات أكتر مِن المطلُوب وزمَايلِها بيحبُّوها.

بكُل تأكِيد هِيَّ مكسَب للشِركة.

وعشان كِدَه مكنش الموضُوع مُفاجأة لمَّا
استدعُوها لِمكتَب رئيستها فِي يُوم مِن الأيَام
الصُبح، وعرضُوا علِيها فُرصة السفر للشُغل فِي
الفرع الرئيسِي للبنك فِي نيويورك.

رندا سَألت رئيستها، نُورا: **"عَايزانِي أسافِر**

وأعِيش وأشتَغل فِي نيويورك؟"

نُورا قَالِت: "أيوة يا راندا. فُرصَة للشغل موجودة وإحنَا شايفِين إنك هتكُوني مِثالية للمنصِب دَه."

"إنتِ مُمتَازة فِي اللِي إنتِ بتعمليه، وإحنَا عَايزِين نِفتح لِيكِي بَاب جدِيد لو تحبّي يعنِي."

الموضُوع مكنش إن راندا مِش عَايزة بس كَانت خَايفة.

لإن دَه معنَاه إنها هتسِيب الأردُن، وعيلتَها وأصنحَابها وتنقِل لِبلد أجنبِي مَتِعْرَفْش فِيه أي حد.

كَانت كُويسة فِي الإنجليِزِي، بس أكيد كَانت مِحتاجَة تاخُد شُوية دُرُوس قبل ماتسَافِر.

راندا قَالِت: "أنا مِش عَارفة أقُول إيه يا نُورا، أنا مُمتنَّة جِدًا على إنك ادتِيني الفُرصة دِي بس أعتقد مِش هقدر أدِيكي جَواب نِهائي دلوقتِي."

"مفِيش مُشكلَة يا راندا خُدِي وقتِك، مِش مطلُوب مِننا نِبعت لِمكتب الفرع الرئيسِي رد رسمِي قبل نِهايِة الأسبوع."

كَان يُوم التّلات، فراندا كَان قُدامهَا تَلَت أيّام

للتفكِير فِي القرار الكِبير دَه.

وشكِرت نُورا وخرجِت مِن مكتبَها.

رِجعِت راندا قعدِت على مكتبَها، وحاولِت تِجمَّع كُل حَاجَة.

بعتِت رِسالة لأعَز أصحابَها عائشة.

راندا بعتِتلها: **"فاضْية النهاردة بعد الشُغل؟، مَكَانًا المُعتاد في كافية بِيت القهوة؟"**

اتهز مُوبايلهَا بعد دقيقتِين. **"أكيد، أشُوفِك هِناك يا راني"**

راندا شَافِت عائشة قاعدة فِي مكَانهُم المُفضَّل فِي الزُكن فِي كافِية بيت القهوة، وقُدامهَا كُبايتِين شَاي. راندا جرِيت عليهَا وقعدِت قُدامهَا.

"شُكرًا إنك قَابلتِيني يا عِيشَة."

عائشة سَألِت: **"مفِيش مُشكِلة يابنتِي، إنتِ كُويسَة؟"**

خدِت راندا نفس عمِيق؛ كَانِت عَارفَة إن عائشة مِش هَيعْجِبْهَا الخبر دَه.

"فِي شُغلِي سألُوني النَهارده لو أحِب أتنقل للشُغل فِي الفرع الرئيسِي فِي نيويورك."

131

عائشة فِضلت ساكتة وبتبُص لراندا.

"و ... أنا مِش عَارفة أستَغِل الفُرصة دِي ولا لأ."

عائشة قَالِت: **"واااو يا راني، دَه مُوضُوع كِبير. أوّلًا وقبل كُل حَاجَة، مبرُوك على إنه جَالِك العرض دَه. ثانِيًا، لأ متزُوجِيش."**

والبنتِين فطسُوا مِن الضِحك فِي نفس اللحظَة.

عائشة قالت: **"أنا بتكلِّم بجد، ماتسبِينِيش!؛ إنتِ أعز أصحابي، هعمِل إيه مِن غِيرِك هِنَا؟"**

ردّت راندا: **"عَارفة، أنا مِش عَارفة بجد أعمِل إيه، وكمَان عيلِتي وأصحَابي هِنا. بس مِن ناحية تانِية هيبقي حلو أوي إني أعِيش فِي أمرِيكا ونيويورك كمَان، ومِش هِيكُون للأبد؛ دِي هتكُون فترة مُؤقتة."**

"أيوة كُلُّهم بيقُولُوا كِدَه، وفِي الأخِر بيتجَوِزُوا مِن أمريكان ويخلِّفُوا عِيال، وعُمرُهم مَا يرجعُوا للأردُن تانِي أبدًا."

ردّت راندا بمَوضُوعِية: **"متقُولِيش كِدَه. أنا عَايزة أكَوِّن أُسرة هِنَا فِي عَمَّان، بس برضُه أنا لسة عندِي سَبعَة وعِشرين سنة. عَايزة أجرب**

اللي الحياة بتعرضُه عليّا."

عائشة شَافِت إن صاحبتَها فِي حِيرة كِبِيرة.

و فكِرت هِيَّ كَانت هتعمل إيه لو كَانِت فِي مكَانها.

أكيد كَانِت هتمِيل للسفر، حتى لو كَان ده مغناه إنها هتسِيب كُل حَاجَة هِنَا وراهَا.

راندا قَالِت: **"لازم أتكلّم مع بابا ومَامَا بالليل. بابا هيعرف إيه اللي المفرُوض يتعمِل، هو دايمًا بِيعرف الصح."**

وبعدين فِي نفس الليلة، لمَّا كَانِت راندا قَاعدة على السُفرَة عشان العشا مع باباها ومامتها وأُختها الصُغيرة، قالت: **"إحِمْ"**، فالعيلة كُلها بصِتلها.

راندا قَالِت: **"عندِي حَاجَة لازم أقُولهالكم كُلكُم."**

عِلي صوت أمَّها و قالت: **"يااااه! قابِلتِي راجِل وهتِتجوِّزِي؟ الحمدُ لِله، أخِيرًا جه اليُوم دَه!"**

أبُوها قال: **"بس يا لينا، سيبِي البِنت تِتكلم."**

"همممم، فِي الحِقيقة لأ. اتعرضِت عليّا وظيفة

مِن شُغلِي النَهارده فِي الفرع الرئيسي فِي نيويورك."

اتغيَّر وِش لينا.

و عِلِي صوتها مرة تانِية: **"إيه؟ لأ، إنتِ بتهزرِي؟. إيه اللِي خلاهُم يفكُروا إنهم مُمكِن يعمِلوا كِدَه؟. هُمَّا مِش عَارفين إن عندِك أُسرة هِنَا، وملكيش حَد فِي أمرِيكا؟!. إيه النَاس السَّخِيفَة دِي؟!"**

راندا قَالِت: **"مَاشِي هيَّ دي المُشكِلة اللِي أنا فِيها، مِش عارفة أعمِل إيه!"**، وبصت لأُختَها اللِي كَانِت بتبُصِلهَا وبتبتِسم.

لينا زعِقِت: **"يعْنِي إيه مِش عَارفة تعمِلي إيه؟!، مينفَعِش تسافرِي إحنَا محتاجِينك هِنَا."**

"إنتِ مِحتاجة تقابِلِي راجِل أرذُني مُحترم وتتجوزِي وتكوِّنِي أُسرة. إنتِ خَلاص بَقى عندِك سَبعَة وعِشرين سنة. أنا كُنت مِتجوِّزة وعندِي طفلِين وأنا قدّك!. قُول حَاجَة يا عَلِي."

والد رُاندا **"عِلِي"** كَان بيحَاوِل يستوعِب كُل حَاجَة. شَكلُه كَان بيفكر، كأنَّه كَان بيحلِّل المَوضُوع وبيقَارِن الإيجَابِيَّات والسلبِيَّات.

علِي سَأَل: **"غَايزة تروحِي أمرِيكا وتاخدِي المنصِب ده يا راندا؟"**

"مِش عَارفة يا بَابا. أعتقد إنِّي نفسِي أرُوح، بس خايفَة برضُه."

لِينا صرخِت: **"علِي! راندا!"** وقَامِت مِن على السُفَرة وسَابِت الأُوضة.

علِي قَال: **"ادِّيها شُوية وقت يا راندا، هيَّ بتحبك جِدًّا، عشَان كِدَه صعب عليها تتخَيل إنك متبقيش عايشة هِنَا بعد كده."**

أمِينة أُخت راندا قَالِت: **"أعتقِد إن المفرُوض تسافِري."**

راندا سَأَلِتها: **"بِجد؟!"**

"طبعًا؛ دِي فُرصة هايلة بالنسبة لِيكِي يا راني، لشغُلِك وكمَان ... لحيَاتِك. دايمًا تقدرِي ترجعِي للأُردُن، بس دلوقتِي سَافرِي وإنتِ لسه قَادرة!"

علِي قَال: **"أنا رأيي زي أُختِك، وعلَى قد مَا هِتوحشِينَا فِي غيابِك سفرِك لأمرِيكا فُرصة مُمَتازة لِيكِي."**

راندا كَان عندَها حَاجَات كِتير تفكر فِيهَا.

فِي اليُوم اللِي بعدُه، خبّطت راندا على بَاب مكتَب رئيسِتهَا.

نُورا قَالِت: **"اتفضلِي يا راندا."**

راندا دخلِت وقعدِت.

وقَالِت: **"شُكرًا يا نُورا، أنا عندِي لِيكي شُوية أسئِلة بالنسبة لنقلِي المُتوقع لنيويورك."**

قَالِت نُورا وهِيَّ مُبتِسمة: **"طبعًا، اتفضلِي."**

راندا سَألِت: **"هحتَاج أسَافِر إمتى؟"**

جَاوِبت نُورا: **"هينحتَاجِك تبدأي فِي بداية الشهر، يعني كمَان تلت أسابِيع."**

راندا قَالِت فِي بالِها: تلت أسابِيع؟ طيب، ده مُمكِن.

راندا سَألِت: **"طيب، هل هِيتكون فِي علَاوة عَلى مُرتِبي؟"**

جَاوِبتها نُورا: **"أكيد طبعًا. بتهَيَّألي إنّي قُلتِلك إمبارِح، بس شكلِي نِسيت. طبعًا هتاخدِي زيادة كبيرة فِي مُرتِبك، وكمَان مُكافأة سنَويَّة والشِركة هِيَّ اللِي هتِدفَع إيجار سكنِك فِي نيويورك.**

وهتاخُد بالهَا مِنك كُويس جِدًا."

راندا قَالِت: "آه تمَام، ده هيفْرق طبْعًا."

نُورا قَالِت: "بِجد يا راندا دِي فُرصة عظِيمة لشَابة زَيك. غَلَط كبير إنك ترفضي الفرصة دي. أنا سافِرت لأمريكا؛ لوس أنجلوس بالتحدِيد لمَّا كُنت فِي سنك وكَانِت دِي أحسن حَاجَة عملتهَا طُول حَياتِي. عِشت هِنَاك سنتِين، واتعلّمت عَن نفسِي أكتر ممَّا كُنت أتوقَّع. قابِلت راجِل أردُني هِنَاك، عشَان كِدَه رجعنا للاستقرَار هِنَا فِي عَمَّان، بس أنا مُمتَنة جِدًا للسنتِين دول."

ابتسِمت راندا. المَوضُوع مِش هَيكون سهل، وأكيد أُمها مِش هَيعجبهَا ده.

بس راندا كَانِت عَايزة تنضَج وكَانِت عَايزة تِبقَى أحسن. عَقلهَا استقَر على قرار، وعِرِفت هِيّ المفرُوض تعِمل إيه.

Vocabulary

هاجِر	to migrate	أمريكا	America
إشتَغَل	to work	خَدَمات مَصرَفِيّة	banking
شِركَة	company	مُوظَّف	employee
زميل	colleague	بِالتأكيد	definitely
أصل	asset	فُرصَة	opportunity
رَوعَة	perfect	أجنَبي	foreign
خايف	afraid	أعتُبِر	to be considered
رِسمي	official	جَواب	response
قَرار	decision	بَعَت إس إم إس	to text (SMS)
حَوِّل	to transfer	أخبار	news
جِدّي	serious	للأبَد	forever
يِتِم إغراؤه	to be tempted	مؤقَّت	temporary
وضَّح	to clear	هَزَّر	to joke

Vocabulary

وَرطة	predicament	عالج	to process
إيجابيّات وسَلبيّات	pros and cons	مِهنة	career
جُهد	potential	مُمكِن يتطبّق	viable
عِلاوَة	bonus	سَنَوي	yearly
رَفَض	to turn down	كان مُمتَن	to be grateful
تَحَدّي	challenging	كبّر	to grow

جاوِب بِصَح أو غَلَظ:

أ) رانْدا إتكَلِّمِت إنجِليزي تُحفَة.

ب) رانْدا كان قُدامْها أسبوع عَشان تِقَرَّر.

ت) عائِشَة كانت عايزَة رانْدا تِقبَل الشُغل.

ث) رانْدا عَندَها سَبعَة وعِشرين سنة.

ج) رانْدا هَتِبدأ شُغلَها الجِديد بَعد تَلَت أسابيع.

كَمِّل الجُمَل:

أ) رانْدا .... شاطرَة في شِركِتها.

ب) رانْدا مَكانِتش عايزَة .... عيلِتها وصْحابها.

ت) .... كان عَندَها طِفلين أمًّا كانِت ....
وعِشرين سَنَة.

ث) نورا عاشِت في .... وقابِلت ....ها
الأردُني هِناك.

إخْتار الإجابة الصَّح:

١.   رانْدا إشتَغَلِت في شِركِتها أد إيه؟

أ)   عَشَر سِنين.

ب)   تَلَت سِنين.

ت)   خَمَس سِنين.

٢.   مَكتَب البَنك الرّئيسي فين؟

أ)   لَندَن.

ب)   عَمَّان.

ت)   نيو يورك.

٣.   إيه الفوايد الزيادَة إللي رانْدا هتاخُدها من شِركِتها؟

أ)   عَرَبيّة شِركَة.

ب)   مُكافئَة شَهريّة.

ت)   مُكافئَة سَنَويّة وإيجار.

NOTES

NOTES

11

حَظ وِحِش

لِينَا رجليها وجعتها من ركُوب العجلة لحد الشُغل.

المسَافة كَانِت تَمانيَة كيلُومتر رايح بس مِن شقتِها لمكتبها فِي وسط عَمَّان.

كَانِت في نُص الطريق، بس امبارِح كَانِت فِي الجِيم، والنهاردة جِسمهَا كُلُه واجِعها.

لِينَا ضغطت على نفسهَا، وفضلِت تبدل، وفكرت: **"أتمنَى كُنت أقدر أشترِي عربِية؛ أي عربِية كَانِت هتقضّي الغرض."**

وصلت لِينَا للشُغل. ولمَّا كَانِت بتقفل عجلِتها،

عدَّى رئيسهَا فِي الشُغل مِن جمبهَا.

رئيسهَا أحمد قَال : **"صبَاح الخِير يا لِينَا، أكيد دِي رِيَاضة جمِيلة بالنسبة ليكي!"**

"أهلًا يا أحمد. أيوة تِقدر تقُول كِده، بس أعتقِد إنِّي جاهزة للعربِية. بركب العجلة مِنْ عِشرين سنة، لو اضطرِّيت أركبها شِتا كمَان ..."

ابتسملهَا أحمد بتعَاطُف ودخل الشُغل.

بعد كِده خِلال اليُوم لمَّا لِينَا كَانت فِي غُرفِة الشَاي، أحمد دخل.

قَرب مِنها وبنبرِة هادية، سألها: **"لِينَا، كُنت بفكر فِي اللي قلتيه النهاردة الصُبح، بخصوص إنك عَايزة عربِية. وفِي الحقيقة، مِرَاتِي بتبِيع عربيتهَا عشَان عَايزة تشترِي واحدة جدِيدة. هِيَّ عربِية قدِيمة فعلًا، بس شغَّالة كُويس جِدًا ويُعتمد عليها وهِيَّ بتبيعها بسعر رخِيص.   مهتمة بحاجة زي كده؟"**

"أوه، شُكرًا على تفكيرك فِيا يا أحمد. مُمكن أسألك هِيَّ هتبيعها بِكَام؟" لِينَا سألِت عشان قلقانة مِن السعر.

"ألفين دِينار بس، بس أنا واثق إننا نِقدر

نخفض مِتين دِينار كمَان عشَانك. خليني أتكَلم مع مراتِي."

"هايل شُكرًا يا أحمد، ابقى عرَّفنِي."

رجعت لِينَا لمكتبهَا فرحانة.

السِعر كَان معقُول فِعلًا بالنسبالهَا، هِيَّ بالفِعل حوِشت ألفين و خُمسُمِيت دِينار عشَان العربِية بس مكِنتش قَادرة تِلاقِي حَاجَة كُويسة بالسِعر دَه.

قبل ما لِينَا ترؤَّح مِن الشُغل فِي اليُوم دَه، أحمد بعتلهَا إيميل بيقول:

"إزيَّك يا لِينَا. اتكلمت مع مراتِي مِن شُوية ووافِقت على بيع العربِية بمبلغ ألف و تُمنُميت دِينار. هل ده مُنَاسِب ليكِي؟. إذا كان مُنَاسِب، أقدر أرتِب إنِّي أجيبلك العربِية بُكره على الشُغل. لو تقدري تدفَعِي عن طرِيق تحويل بنكِي يبقى كويس أوي، عرفِيني. شُكرًا، أحمد."

كتبت لِينَا الرد:

"أهلًا يا أحمد، دَه شيء مُمتَاز. لو سمحت عرَّف مِراتك إنِّي عَايزة أشترِي العربِية مِنهَا. هحوِّلَّها الفلُوس بُكرَه. شُكرًا مرة تانية يا أحمد، دِي بجد

مُساعدة كبيرة جِدًا!. لِينَا."

وصلت لِينَا للشُغل اليُوم اللي بعدُه الصُبح بدرِي.

وكَانِت جت بتاكسي عالشُغل. كان إحساس جمِيل إنها تحِس إنهَا مِش مُضطرة تِركب عجلة تانِي للشُغل بعد النَهاردة.

مِشيِت وزا المبنى وشَافِت أحمد بيركِن فِي موقف العربيَّات عربِية قدِيمة شُوية، بس لسَّه شكلها حلو.

نزِل مِن العربِية وشَاف لِينَا.

أحمد قَال وهُوَّ بيلف المفَاتِيح فِي الهوَا: **"بقِت بتاعتِك!"**

لِينَا شَبَكت إيديها فِي بعض من الفرحة. وراحت عالعربِية وفتحِت بَاب السَواق.

دخلِت وقعدِت عالكُرسِي. ريحتها مِن جُوَّه برفَان.

العربِية مِن جُوَّه كَانِت قدِيمة شُوية (مُوديل ألفين و واحِد)، بس لِينَا شافِت إنها حلوة بالنسبالهَا.

لِينَا قَالِت: **"أنا حبتها يا أحمد، هحول الفلُوس لمرَاتك النَهارده. لو سمحت ابعتِلي إيميل بالتفاصِيل."**

148

عَلى مدار أسبوعِين، سَاقِت لِينَا عربيتها فِي كُل مكَان. وهِيَّ حبِت إنها تكون حُرَّة.

راحِت لبيت أهلها فِي الغرب، وزارِت أختها فِي الشرق.

وهِيَّ وصاحبتها حتى راحُوا للشَّظ فِي أجازة أخرالأسبُوع.

فِي يُوم مِن الأيَّام الصُبْح وهي فِي طريقِها للشُغل، لِينَا اتزنقت فِي زحمة المُرُور فِي ساعة الذُروَة الغير طبيعية فِي عَمَّان.

وهي ماشية واحدة واحدة، مع الوقوف والحركة لِينَا سمِعت صُوت مُضجِك.

كَان صوت غريب طالع من عربيتها.   وفجأة، العربِية نطت لقُدام وبطلِت فِي نُص الشارِع.

لِينَا لفت المفَاتيح وحاولِت تشَغلها مرة تانية، بس مشتغلتش.

فِضلت بس تعِمل صُوت التدوير. لِينَا قَالِت فِي عقلها: **"يا ربِّي."**

"هعمِل إيه؟" العربِيات اللي وراها كَانُوا كُلهُم بيضربوا كلاكس.

149

لِينَا حسّت بالخُوف، وبصت وراهَا لقت طابُورعربِيات طويِل.

"أعمِل إيه؟... استنِي ... فاكرة لمَّا عربِية بَابا عِطلت وإنتِ صُغيرة. كان عمل إيه ساعِتهَا؟ ... آه صح! كان شغَّل نُور الانتِظَار." ودورِت لِينَا على الزُرار الأحمر اللِي عليه شكل مُثلث.

ضغطِت عليه وإشارَات العربِية الاتنين اشتغلُوا. **"طيب، دلوقتِي إيه؟"** نزلِت مِن العربِية ورفعت كِتفها للعربِيات اللِي وراهَا.

راجِل مِن العربِيات دِي نِزل وجالها.

سألهَا: **"عربِيتك عِطلت يا آنِسة؟"**

سألتُه: **"أيوة، أعمل إيه؟"**

"اركبِي العربِية، وأنا هزُقَّك وعايزِك توجِّهِي العربِية على جمب الطرِيق."

لِينَا رِكبت، والراجل بدأ يزق ضهر عربِيتها.

حوْدت الدريكسِيُون فِي اتجاه على جنب الطرِيق، والعربِية بدأت تتحرك ببُطء. وأخيرًا لمَّا العربِية بعدِت عن الطرِيق، عدتها العربِيات التانية بسُرعة.

نزلِت مرة تانية. **"شُكرًا يا أستاذ، أخُويا ميكَانيكِي**

150

هتِصل بيه."

الراجِل ابتسم وشاورلها، ورجع لعربيته ومِشى.

لِينَا طلَّعِت تليفُونهَا مِن شنطِتها وطلِبت رقم أخُوها جمَال.

قَالِت: **"إزيك يا جمَال، مِحتاجة مُساعدِتك. عربِيتي الجدِيدة عِطلت على الطرِيق السرِيع."**

جمَال قَال: **"بِجد؟ حظِك وِحش. ابعتيلِي مكانِك بالظَبط وهحَاوِل أكُون عندِك فِي تَلاتين دقيقة."**

لِينَا بعتِت الرسالة لجمَال، وبعدين اتصلت بمكتبهَا. مُوظفة الاستقْبال ردت عَلى التليفُون.

"أهلًا يا مارا، أنا لِينَا. عربِيتي عِطلت وأنا فِي طرِيقي للشُغل، فهتأخر النهَارده."

ردت عليها مُوظفة الاستقْبال: **"إزيِّك يا لِينَا، معلِش . شُكرًا إنك اتصلِتي وعرفتِيني، هَوَصل الرِسالة لأحمد."**

لِينَا استنت. جمَال كَان عندُه حق، أكيد ده شُوء حظ. هِيِّ اشترت العربِية مِن أسبُوعِين بس!.

فكرِت فِي عقلها إنها كَان لازِم تودّي العربِية للصِيانة، كَان لازِم تكشِف عليها قبل ما تشترِيهَا.

151

عربية بدأت تِزمَّر. كَان جمَال، وركن ورَا عربيتَها.

لِينَا قالت بصوت عالي: **"الحمدُ لله!. جمَال أنا معندِيش أي فِكرة إيه المُشكلة فِي العربِية دِي!"**

نزل جمَال مِن عربيتُه. **"خلِينَا نبُص."**

مشي ناحية وِش العربِية وفتح الكبُّوت، وفِضل يبُص جُواها حوالِي عَشر دقَايق ويحرك حَاجَات هِنَا وهِنَاك.

"لِينَا، شكلها كِده فِي مُشكلَة فِي المُولّد."

قَالت لِينَا فِي عقلها: **"أيّا كان اللِي بتقوله ..."**

"هضطر أكلم الصنايعية بتُوعِي عشان نِسحب العربِية عالورشَة. ونشتغَل فِيها هِنَاك. أعتقد هتفضل معانَا لمُدِة أربَعْ أيام."

فِي اليُوم اللِي بعدُه، لمَّا ركبت لِينَا عجلِتها للشُغل، كَانِت فِي الواقع مُمتنَّة؛ مُمتنَّة لعجلِتها اللِي تستحق الثِقة.

قَالت لِينَا فِي عقلها: **"على الأقل مش هتِعطل."**

Vocabulary

عَرَبيّة	car	باظ	to break down
رِكِب عَجَلَة	to cycle	رجول	legs
وَجَع	to hurt	كيلومِتر	kilometre
إمبارِح	yesterday	جيم	gym
كَشّر	to grimace	وَجَع	to ache
ضَغَط عَلَى البَدّال	to pedal	قِدِر يِدفَع	to afford
موتوسيكل	bike	قَفَل	to lock
غَدَّى	to walk past	تَمرين	exercise
شِتا	Winter	جاهِز	ready
بِتَعاطُف	sympathetically	أوضية الشاي	tea room
إشتَرَى	to buy	باع	to sell
رِخيص	cheap	مَوثوق فيه	reliable
سِعر	price	كان مُهتّم	to be interested

153

VOCABULARY

كان مُهتَّم	to be concerned	كان في مُنتهَى السعادَة	to be delighted
كان بيحوّش فِلوس	to save (money)	كان قادِر	to be able
إيميل	email	وافِق	to agree
رَتَّب	to arrange	حِوالة بَنكيّة	bank transfer
مِشي	to walk	رَن	to jingle
سَلَّم	to clasp	سوّاق	driver
بَرفان	perfume	حِساب	account
شَرق	east	تَفاصيل	details
بَحر	beach	ساق	to drive
وِقِف	to stop	حُريّة	freedom
إزعاج	noise	غَرب	west
شخَّر	to grunt	زُعب	panic
إتهَّز	to jerk	أنوار الخَطَر	hazard lights

VOCABULARY

بِشَكل مُفاجِئ	abruptly	زُرار	button
إنتّهَز	to jiggle	مُثلَّث	triangle
الهَسهَسَة	hissing	مؤشِرات	indicators
بوق	horn	هَّز كِتافُه	to shrug
صَفَّر بالمُزمار	to honk	أكتاف	shoulders
تَدوير	to steer	عَجَلة	wheel
ظريق سَريع	highway	جَنب	side
حَظ	luck	ظريق	road
رِسالَة	message	حَرَّك	to move
خِدمَة	service	ميكانيكي	mechanic
راجِع	to check	رَقَم	number
غَلَط	wrong	بونيه	bonnet
مولِّد تيّار بَديل	alternator	قَرَص	to tweak

155

Vocabulary

سحَب	to tow	يُعتَمد عَليه	trustworthy
جَراج	garage	فِكرة	idea

جاوِب بِصَح أو غَلَظ:

أ)   المَسافة نُص كيلو مِن بيت لينا للشُغْل.

ب)   لينا بِتسوق عَجَلِتها بَقالها عِشرين سَنَة.

ت)   لينا دَفَعِت ألفين وخُمسُميت دينار لِلعَرَبيّة.

ث)   لينا وصاحِبتها ساقوا لِغاية البحر في العَرَبيّة الجديدة.

ج)   مُبَرِّد العَرَبيّة كان بايظ.

كَمِّل الجُمَل:

أ)   ضوء .... أحمَر وعَليه ....

ب)   لينا كانِت .... عَشان مكانِتش هتحتاج إنَّها يِتسوق .... تاني.

ت)   .... و .... لينا عايشين في الغَرب وأختَها عايشة في ....

ث)   لينا .... العَجَلَة للناحِية التانيَة من الطريق.

إخْتار الإجابة الصَّح:

١. إيه فَصل السَنة دِلوَقتي؟

أ) صيف.

ب) شِتا.

ت) رَبيع.

٢. أحْمَد بيقتَرِح إنُّه يِدفَع لِلينا

أ) نَقدي.

ب) شيك.

ت) حِوالة بنكيّة.

٣. أخو لينا بيشتَغَل إيه؟

أ) دُكتور.

ب) مُهَندِس.

ت) ميكانيكي.

NOTES

NOTES

12

اليوم المُنتَظَر

نُور كَانت قابِلت كرِيم مِن سِت شهُور فِي مُؤتمر فِي عَمَّان.

أقل حاجة نقدر نقولها عنُه، إنُّه كان حُب مِن أول نظرة.

نُور عُمرها أبدًا ما حسّت بارتِباط قوي مع أي إنسَان تانِي زي ما حسّت مع كرِيم.

الاتنِين كَانُوا دكاترة وهُمَّا الاتنِين بيحِبُوا الأكل الحلو، والخُرُوج وكُورِة القدم.

هُوَّ كان بيهَدِّيهَا وهِيَّ كَانِت مُتَحَمِسَة جدًا. عشَان كِدَه لمَّا كرِيم اتقدِّملها، نُور ماتفجئِنْش،

بس كَانِت مبسُوطة جِدًا.

وكُونُه مصرِي اتولد فِي أمرِيكا، كَان كرِيم جدِيد عليه كُل العَادات والتقَاليد الأرْدُنِية، بس كَان أكتر مِن مبسُوط عشان هيتعرَّف أكتر على الحَاجَات دِي وكَان مُتحمِّس جِدًا عشان يبدأ حَيَاتُه مع نُور.

نُور سأَلِت: **"طيب، إحنا عندِنا حفلِة الخُطوبة وحفلِة العشَا الأسبُوع الجاي. إنت جاهِز؟"**

ضِحك كرِيم: **"أعتقد أه. إيه اللِي هيكُون صعب يعنِي؟"**

سكِتِت نُور. مش مسأَلِة صعُوبة، بس نُور كَانِت بتتمنى إن كرِيم ميبقَاش متأثر جِدًا.

كَانِت بتتخيِّل إن دخُولُه فِي عِيلة أردُنِية مُمكِن يكُون صَعب شُوية بالنِسباله.

عشان فِي أفراد كتير جِدًا فِي العيلة، وعادات وتقاليد جدِيدة يتعوَّد عليهَا.

بس مكنش عندها شك إن كرِيم قد المسئُولية. وفِي الأخِر بعد كُل شيء، هتِتجوزه.

وفِي يُوم الخمِيس اللِي بعده، وصلَت نُور ومعَاها كرِيم لبيت أسرة نُور.

أمَّها وأبُوها رحبُوا بِيهُم كتير، وكانوا مركزين مع كرِيم.

بُناءًا على التقَالِيد، أسرة كرِيم كَان المفرُوض يكُونُوا هِنا برضُه، بس عشَان هُمَّا خطَّظُوا يتجوِزُوا فِي الأردُن، فأسرته قررِت تِيجي فِعلًا مِن أمرِيكا على معاد الجَواز.

دخلُوا بِيت أسرة نُور ودخلُوا على الصَالة. كَانِت أخت نُور وبنت عمهَا وأعز أصحابهَا موجُودِين هِنَاك، بالإِضافة إلى عدد مِن الشبَاب أصحَاب كرِيم مِن الشُغل.

سلَّمُوا كُلُّهُم على بعض، ونُور وأمها زارا قعدُوا على كنبة مع البِسِتّات، وكرِيم وأبو نُور "محمد" قعدُوا على كنبة تانية مع الرِّجَّالة.

"طيب، أنا سعِيد جِدًا إننا اتجمعْنا كُلّنا هِنَا النهَاردة فِي التجمُّع الغِير رسمِي ده. يا كرِيم، أنا وأم نُور حابين نرحب بيك فِي العيلة. وإحنا مُتحمسِين جِدًا إن بقى عندِنا حد أجنبي فِي الأسرة." وضحِك محمد.

ضِحك كُل اللِي قاعدِين برضُه وبصت نُور لكرِيم وغمزِتلُه.

كِريم قال: "إحم."

كِريم قَال: "شُكرًا لِيكُم يا محمد ويا زارا. أنا مُتحمِس جِدًا إنى أتجوِز بِنتكُم، وهِيَّ بتخلِّيني سعِيد جِدًا." وبص لنُور وابتسم، ونُور ابتسِمِتلُه.

"وأنا باخُد إذنكُم إنتُوا الاتنِين رسمِي إني أتجوِز نُور."

ابتسم أبُو نُور وأمها وهما بِيهزوا راسهُم لكَريم.

طلَّع عِلبة صُغيرة مِن جيبُه، وقدَّم كِريم لنُور هدِية الخُطُوبة التقلِيدية. قبلت نُور الهدِية وفتحِت العِلبة.

كَانِت عِبارة عن حلَق ألماظ جمِيل. نُور قَالِت: "شُكرًا يا كِريم، عجبني جِدًا."

بعد كِدَه اتبادلُوا خوَاتِم الخُطُوبة - دِبَل دهبِ بسِيطة - ولبِّسُوهَا لبعض فِي الصباع الوسظانِي التاني مِن إيديهم اليمِين.

قال محمد بصوت عالي: "مبرُوك عليكُم. دلوقتِي، يلا خلُّونا ناكُل."

نُور لفت للبِنَات، اللي كُلُهم حضنُوهَا وباسُوهَا

164

وأمها حضِنتِها جَامِد.

قَالِت وهي بتبص على فاطمة أخت نُور: **"مِين كَان يصدق إن بِنتِي الصغيرة تِتجوِز قبل أختها الكِبِيرة."**

ابتسِمت فاطمة لأمها: **"أعتقد نُور قابِلت الراجِل المُناسِب ليها قبلِي يا ماما!"**

واتجمعُوا كُلُّهم على السُفرَة اللِي كَانِت مليانة أكل مستنِينهُم.

كَان فِي طعمية، وحُمُّص، ولبنة، وتبُّولة، وسلَطة، وأنواع مُختلِفة مِن اللُحُوم والرُز والحلويَّات.

أكلُوا وضحكُوا وعلى آخر العشَا، كَان كرِيم حاسِس وكَإِنُه واحِد مِن الأسرة.

أربع شهُوَر عدُّوا، وصحيت نُور أخِيرًا على يُوم فرحهَا وكَانِت مُتوتِرة جِدًا.

أختها وأصحابها هِيوصلوا بعد شوية صغيرين عشَان يساعدُوهَا تِجهز. صحِيت وقَامِت تاخُد دُش.

وفِي نفس الوقت فِي الجَمب التاني مِن المدِينة كَان كرِيم بيعْمِل نفس الخَاجَة. أصحابه

هِيَوصلوا بعد شوية برضُه.

وكَان أبُوه وأمه جُم مِن أمرِيكا بقَالُهُم يُومِين، وقاعدِين فِي فُنْدُق فِي المدينة قُرب المطعم اللِي هَيِتعمل فِيه الفرح.

شُوية مِن أصحابُه مِن أمرِيكا برضُه جُم للأردُن عشان اليُوم الكِبير دَه، وكَان مُتحمّس جِدًا إنُه يشُوف الكُل.

وبعد الضُهر، وصل العرِيس والعرُوسة بيت أهل نُور. كَان البيت مِنور بكُل أنواع الإضَاءةَ اللِي كَانِت مِتعلقَة على المبنَى مِن بَرَه.

كَانِت تقَالِيد عربية، وكَان شكله حلو جِدًا.

كَانِت أسرة نُور وأصحابها قاعدِين على جمب في الصَالة، وأسرة كرِيم وأصحَابُه كَانُوا قاعدِين على الجمب التانِي.

كرِيم قعد قُدام الكُل، وكَانِت فِي مُوسِيقى عربية شغالة والحلويات بِتِتوزع علَى الضُيوف. وفجْأة وقفِت المُوسِيقى وبدأت مُوسِيقى الفرح التقلِيدية بدلهَا.

دخلِت نُور وأبُوها الصَالة وقعدُوا. كرِيم سيطر عليه الصمت. كَانِت أول مرة يشُوف نُور جمِيلة أوي كِدَه.

وبمُجرد ما خلصُوا توقِيع عقُود الجواز، قرب كرِيم مِن نُور وباسها على راسها.

هُمَّا الاتنِين نقلُوا دِبلهُم مِن إيديهم اليمِين للصباع الوسطانِي التانِي فِي إيدِيهم الشِمال. بعد الحفلة كُل الضُيوف راحُوا على المطعم عشان الاستقبال.

نُور وكرِيم فَضلُوا شُوية.

نُور سألِت: **"وااو، خلاص كده!. حاسِس بإيه يا كرِيم؟"**

كرِيم قَال: **"إحساس جمِيل. إنتِ كُنتِ جَمِيلة"** ومَال نحيِتها يبُوسهَا.

نُور كَان نِفسهَا اللحظة دِي تستمر للأبد، بس برضُه كَانِت عَارفة إن وزاهُم مواعِيد.

دخلُوا العربية اللِي كَانِت مستنيَّاهُم قُدام البِيت، وفِي الطرِيق للمطعم، مِسك كرِيم إيد نُور.

كرِيم قَال: **"أنا مبسُوط جِدًا إِني زُحت المُؤتمر، وقررت أخُد الوظِيفة فِي مُستشفَى عَمَّان، كُل دَه جمعِني بيكِي."**

نور كان قلبها طاير من الفرحة.

وصلُوا للمطعم، اللِي كَان فخم جِدًا. كَان سقفه عالِي والأرضيَّات كُلها رُخَام.

وكَان الديكُور لُونُه كرِيمي، وكُل التجهِيَزات كَانِت معمُولة مِن وَرِدِي على دهِبِي. دخلُوا جُوه والكُل بدأ يهتِفلهُم.

أصحابُهُم وأُسرهُم كَانُوا كُلهُم قاعدِين على ترابِيزَات مدورة، واشتغلِت المُوسِيقى.

الأكل والمشرُوبَات كَانِت جَاية، ومَنطِقة الرقص كَانِت جاهزة.

وتم الترحِيب بكرِيم ونُور بأول رقصة ليهُم كزُوج وزُوجة. أخذ كرِيم نُور بين إيديه واشتغلِت أغنِيتَها العربية المُفضَّلة.

رقصُوا ببُطء، وهُمَّا بيبتسْمُوا فِي وِش بعض بسعَادة.

لمَّا خلصِت الأغِنية نادُوا على الكُل عشان يِجوا يرقصوا، وساعِتها بدأت المُتعة الحقِيقية.

رقصَات مِن جمِيع الأنوَاع، وكُل واحِد كَان عنُده الشجاعة الكافية يرقُص.

كرِيم ونُور خذُوا خطوة لوَرا، وشافُوا كُل النَاس اللِي فِي حياتُهم بيرقصُوا ويستمتِعُوا بالحياة.

كِريم قَال: **"دلوقتي هُوَّ دَه الاحتِفَال الحَقيقي، عيلتك بِكُل تأكِيد بتعرف إزاي تعِيش الحياة وتحتفِل."**

ابتسمت نُور، وكَانِت سعِيدة جِدًا إن كُل حَاجَة مِشيِت تمَام، وإن كِريم اندمج بشكل كبير مع حياتَها وعيلتها وثقافتهَا بسهُولة.

خدِت إيده ومِسكِتها جَامِد، وكُلها حمَاس لِلي هِيَقدمُه ليهم الجُزء الجَاي مِن حياتُهُم.

169

Vocabulary

إتجَوّز	to marry	مؤتَمَر	conference
حُب	love	عَمّان	Amman
تَقليل أهَمية	understatement	قَوي	strong
إنسان	human	إتصال	connection
بَرّة	outdoors	كورة	football
هِدي	to calm	طَلّع شَرارة	to spark
مَصري	Egyptian	طاقة	energy
مَولود	born	إتقَدّم	to propose
عادة	custom	إتفاجِئ	to be surprised
عُرف	tradition	مُتعِب	daunting
مَراسيم	ceremony	أعضاء	members
حَفلة	party	إتعَوّد	to get accustomed
إرتَبَك	overwhelmed	شَك	doubt
أولياء أمر	parents	غَمَز	to wink

VOCABULARY

هَنّى	to greet	إذن	permission
تَقليدي	traditional	هِديّة	gift
دَخَل	to enter	ماسة	diamond
مِش رَسمي	informal	حُلقان	earrings
تَجَمُّع	gathering	خاتِم	ring
أجنَبي	foreigner	دَهَب	gold
نُص	middle	يمين	right
مَبروك	congratulations	باس	to kiss
سَلَطة	salad	عَصَر	to squeeze
لَحمَة	meat	رُز	rice
حَلَويّات	sweets	فَراشات	butterflies
عَروسة	bride	عَريس	groom
مُبِهر	impressive	ضيف	guest
موسيقى	music	قانوني	legal

Vocabulary

سَقف	ceiling	أرض	floor
رُخام	marble	لون	color
تَجهيزات	fittings	كِريمَة	cream
فِرِح	to cheer	رَقَص	to dance

جاوِب بِصَح أو غَلَظ:

أ)   الفَرَح كان بَعد خَمَس شُهور مِن حَفلِة الخُطوبَة.

ب)   كَريم مُهَندِس ونور مُدَرِّسَة.

ت)   العَرَبيّة كانِت مِستَنيّاهم قُدّام البيت.

ث)   ديكور المَظعَم كان لون كِريمي وفَرش دَهَبي.

ج)   كَريم أردُني بَس اتوَلَد في أمْريكا.

كَمِّل الجُمَل:

أ)   المَطعَم .... كان عالي وأرضُه كانِت ....

ب)   البيت كان .... بِسبب كُل الأنوار.

ت)   الموسيقى الـ......... كانِت شَغَّالَة و .... كانِت بِتتقَدَّم لـ......... .

ث)   نور قابلِت كَريم من .... شُهور في .... في عَمّان.

173

إخْتار الإجابة الصَّح:

١. حَفلِة الخُطوبَة كانِت في أي يوم في الأسبوع؟

أ) إتنين.

ب) سَبت.

ت) خَميس.

٢. إيه الهِدية اللي كَريم إدَّاها لِنور؟

أ) خَاتِم ذَهب.

ب) عُقد أبيَض في ذَهبي.

ت) حَلَق ألماظ.

٣. كَريم عَمَل إيه بَعد ما وقَّع عَلَى الوَرَق؟

أ) مِسِك إيد نور.

ب) باس نور عَلَى راسها.

ت) شَكَر أبو نور.

NOTES

NOTES

TRANSLATIONS

Translator's note: *We've tried to keep these translations as close to the Arabic text as possible. However in some cases, loose translations were necessary.*

Family

My name is Fatima, and I am eight years old, I live in my home with my mum, my dad, and my baby brother Amir. He is only one year old and loves to play with me. This morning I carry Amir to the table for breakfast, and Dad offers me some of his coffee.

"Yuck!" I say, and my father laughs at me.

He drinks coffee every day at breakfast time, but I think it smells bad and tastes even worse.

"Would you like some jam on your bread, Fatima?" asks my mother.

"Yes please!" I tell her, "and Amir would like some too!"

"Okay," says mum, and she puts a few pieces of bread on a plate for my brother and me. When she brings it to us, I watch Amir play with his bread instead of eating it, and it makes me happy. My father gives us all a kiss goodbye as he goes to work, and I stay at the table with Amir to eat our breakfast. He likes to make a mess and Mum has to clean it up. I laugh as she wipes the jam off his cheeks.

I finish my breakfast and go outside to play with my friend, I

have to walk down the street to find my friend Hawa. She has black hair and brown eyes like I do, but she is much taller than me. When I get to her house her big brother calls out to me, he has a big smile on his face,

"Hello, Fatima!" He says.

"Hello!" I say.

"Are you looking for Hawa?" He asks.

"Yes, I want to see if she wants to play with me," I tell him.

"HAWA!" He yells.

"COMING!" She says, and she rushes to the door.

"Good morning Hawa, would you like to come and play?"

"Yes please!" She says and smiles at me.

We wave goodbye to her big brother and run into the street. It is sunny outside, and we find our ball to play with. The street is full of people and other children playing. Hawa and I kick the ball to each other almost all morning. We always have a lot of fun together when we play, and it makes me sad to have to go home.

When I get home, Amir is fast asleep, and I see that my mother is starting to make bread in the kitchen. "Can I help?" I ask her.

"Of course," she says, and gives me a big bowl and spoon. In the bowl, we put flour and water and I get to mix it all together.

"Dad will love his fresh bread when he gets home," she tells me.

"To have with smelly coffee," I say.

She laughs at me and shows me how to finish making the bread. I love to make bread with my mum, and I get to eat the first piece when it is cooked. I think the first piece always tastes the best!

A Special Meal

It is Samira's birthday, and so she decides to take her family to dinner at her favorite restaurant. Samira's favorite is a Shawarma restaurant near her home, so she says that they should all walk. Samira has a small family, her husband Asad, and her two children Omar, and Eman. Her children are 2 years old and 5 years old, so she must take a pram for little Eman.

When they arrive at the restaurant, Omar runs to a table near the window. He likes this table most because he can look at the garden outside. Asad takes Eman out of the pram and puts her in a special seat so she can reach the table like her brother does.

"What would everyone like to eat tonight?" Asks the waiter. He has a pen and paper to write everything down.

"Bread!" Yells Eman, and claps her hands.

"Falafel please," says Omar.

"We will have the special please," says Samira, she likes all of the food here.

"Alright," says the waiter, "it won't be very long, would you like me to bring you some juice?"

"Yes please," says Samira "everyone will have some."

Samira likes this restaurant so much because she used to come here when she was a child, her mother would feed her bread with hummus. Samira would steal pieces of everyone's food as well because she couldn't choose a favorite. Now that she is grown up she lets her children eat whatever they like too.

Eman is too little to eat much food, so she eats bread and hummus like Samira used to. She also gets to drink juice which is her favorite treat. Omar likes to eat falafel most, and he is usually the first one to finish dinner because he eats so fast. Asad likes to let Samira choose for him because he likes to make Samira happy.

"Here is your juice," says the waiter and gives everyone their juice.

"Thank you," says Samira. She helps Eman drink some.

"I played with Muhammad at school today, mum," says Omar.

"That's nice, what did you play?" She asks.

"Hide and seek!" He says, "Muhammad is very good at hiding."

"You're good at hiding too," says Asad, and smiles at Omar.

He smiles back at his father, Asad had taught him how to play Hide and Seek, and so Omar taught his friends. His favorite part of the game is counting to fifty when his friends hide.

When the food comes, everyone starts to eat, and talk about all

the things that they did that day.

Samira stayed home with Eman, and they read stories. Asad went to work and was very busy all day. Omar went to school with his friends, and they all had fun. The food is delicious and gets eaten very fast.

Samira gets a big surprise when Asad and the children surprise her with presents and sing the birthday song. She loves this restaurant because it makes her family so happy, and she loves her family very much.

Talented People

My name is Amal, and my favorite hobby is painting and drawing. I love to paint and draw all kinds of things. My favorite picture I have made is of my family. I painted me, my big sisters, and my dad in front of our house.

I like to use the color blue a lot when I paint because it is my favorite color. It is like the sky. I like to paint nearly every day, and painting animals is my favorite, today I am going to paint a yellow camel with brown sand a big blue sky. I hope everyone will like my painting.

One day I would like to do a big painting on a wall like the ones I see in the streets, I want to make people happy with my paintings.

I have a friend named Muhammed, and he likes to cook! When I visit him, he will always cook for me.

"What are you going to cook today Muhammed?" I ask him. "Today I will make tabbouleh," he says, and he starts to mix the food.

I like to watch Muhammed cook, but the art I like the best is eating the food when he has finished making it. Muhammed's mum teaches him how to cook lots of different things, and he helps her to make dinner every day. I think that it would be a lot of fun to be able to cook as well as my friend Muhammed.

Our friend Angelina is very good at basketball, and she helps me to learn it. I am not as good as she is, but she plays all the time to

become even better. One day I think she'll be good enough to win a game in a special team!

"My favorite thing about basketball is throwing the ball through the hoop," says Angelina. She shows me how to throw the ball through the hoop, but I can't do it yet.

"It took me a long time to learn how to do it at first too," she tells me, "but if you keep trying one day you will be able to!"

It makes me happy to have such a kind friend.

We have a friend who likes to play guitar, and his name is Shady. We love to listen to Shady play his guitar, and we even sing along to some of the songs. Shady is very good at playing the guitar, and he knows a lot of songs.

Shady says his dad taught him how to play and even gave him his very own guitar for his birthday. Now that Shady has his own guitar he brings it lots of places with him and plays music for all of his friends.

Even though we all have different hobbies, we are all best friends! We like to learn about each other's' hobbies, it's lots of fun to learn new things. I really hope I never stop learning new things.

Mom's Day Out

This is Nadia, and today is going to be a fun day for her, she has been invited to a friend's wedding, and she needs something nice to wear. Nadia and her friend have known each other since they were very young, so she is very happy for her friend. Nadia is looking forward to shopping because not only does she get to catch up with another friend of hers, she gets to leave the kids home and have a day to herself! Nadia does her makeup and heads outside to wait for her friend, Amira, who will take them to the shopping center. Her car pulls up, and Nadia gets in the passenger side.

"I'm so excited," Nadia tells Amira.

"Me too!" She replies, and they begin to drive to the store, "how are the kids?"

"Not so good!" she says, "they've been sick all week, and I have

barely slept!"

"That's no good, I hope they are feeling better soon the poor dears!" Amira says, and turns on the radio.

The friends sing along to their favorite songs to occupy them for the long drive. When they reach the shop the pair decide to go a formal wear store first.

"There are so many choices!" says Nadia, she feels a little overwhelmed.

"I know isn't it fabulous?" says Amira, she loves shopping and rushes straight over to the first rack to start looking at dresses.

"Where do I even start?" Nadia asks with a laugh.

"Well, why don't you look for some colors you like and start there?" Amira suggests. Nadia goes over to a rack that has several blue dresses hanging on it. Blue is her favorite color so she decides to pick a few in her size.

"Let's go try these on!" Amira says, she is very excited and has about five choices of dress.

Nadia and Amira go into the change rooms and try on their first dress, Amira has chosen a short red dress, and Nadia tries on a flowy light blue one. They come out from the stalls to show each other.

"I really like that one!" Amira tells Nadia, "it really suits you!"

"I think yours is a bit short," Nadia says, and they change into their next choices. This time Nadia has a dark blue dress that comes just past her knee and Amira has a pink dress with ruffles on the shoulder. Amira walks out laughing because the ruffles are getting in her face.

"I look ridiculous!" she says, and Nadia has to agree.

"I feel like this is a dress I would wear to work, not a wedding!" Nadia laughs, she is beginning to have some fun.

So they go into the change rooms again, and Nadia puts on her last dress. It is a very long dress, and she has trouble walking out. Amira has on a sweet green dress that matches her eyes.

"I love that one!" says Nadia, "it makes your eyes look so pretty!"

"Thank you!" says Amira, "I think the first one you tried on was

my favorite, though."

"Mine too," Nadia says, and they go to change back into their regular clothes.

At the counter, Amira pays for her green dress and also decides to buy a silver necklace that she hides from Nadia. Nadia takes the first dress up to the counter.

"Now we need shoes!" Amira says and takes Nadia by the hand to pull her into the next shop.

Nadia is laughing, and nearly drops her bag.

"Hey slow down," she says.

"No, shoes are my favorite part," says Amira, and they enter the shoe shop.

"I don't like wearing high heels," Nadia complains.

"You can choose flat ones then," Amira replies.

Nadia decides to go over to the sales table and look there. She finds a nice pair of grey shoes that she thinks are very comfortable, and decides to choose those in case she is running after her kids all day.

"Do the kids need shoes too?" asks Amira, holding up a cute pair of girl's sandals.

"Oh, I'm sure she would love those! Thank you," says Nadia and takes the sandals for her daughter.

For her son, she decides on some black dress shoes and takes everything to the counter. Amira has chosen a pair of white high heeled sandals.

"I couldn't even walk in those," says Nadia. They both pay for their shoes, and Nadia says she had better pick out something for the kids to wear too.

When they get to the children's store Nadia picks a cute white dress for her daughter, it has some bright colored flowers sewn into it which will make her daughter very happy. For her son, she picks a little t-shirt that looks like a suit top and a pair of small black jeans.

"They are going to look adorable!" Amira says.

"More adorable than they do this week, they look awful," Nadia

laughs.

"I hope they don't get you sick for the wedding" Amira laughs and suggests they get some coffee to drink on the way home.

"I think we deserve it," says Nadia, so they go and order their drinks and head for the car.

"I am exhausted!" Amira says.

"Me too," says Nadia, "I hope dinner is ready for me when I get home, I am starving!"

"That would be nice!" says Amira, "you had better say hello to the kids for me because I don't want them to make me sick!"

"That's probably a good idea," says Nadia, "thank you so much for coming with me today, I usually hate shopping, but it was a lot of fun to come with you!"

"That's alright," says Amira, "any time you need somebody to come with you I will. You know how much I love to shop!"

Nadia laughs. "See you at the wedding!"

"See you there! Have a good night, I hope your little ones feel better by then," Amira says, dropping Nadia back home.

Italy

My name is Waleed, I am 13 years old, and I have 6 brothers and sisters. We all live together in a little house on a busy street. It is a Tuesday morning, and I am walking to school like I do every day. I like going to school because I get to see my friends and learn about new things, my favorite subject is maths.

The reason I like maths so much is that I love to understand how numbers work, and how to write equations. It also helps me to learn about money. I enjoy the walk to school because it gives me some alone time away from my big family. I think it will be a hot day today because the sun is already hot against my skin, and I am getting thirsty already. I will have a drink from my water bottle when I get to school, I always keep one in my bag. The road to school is long, so I have to leave early in the morning and walk through the busy streets.

When I get to school, I go to my classroom, it is shady and cool inside. I open my backpack to find my water bottle, but it's gone! I feel upset and very thirsty. I sit down at my desk and wait for my friend to come, my other classmates arrive and sit down at their desks, but my friend doesn't come. I think he must be sick because Asad likes coming to school as much as I do.

Today will be a lonely day, Asad is my best friend, and I don't have any others because I am new to this school. When my teacher comes, she tells us we are going to be doing a reading, so we all take out our books so we can take turns to read aloud. When my turn arrives, a boy in the back laughs at me because I have trouble saying some of the words. It makes me feel very sad to be made fun of, and I want to stop reading. My teacher smiles at me and tells me to keep trying, so I do. When I get to the end of my part, the boy laughs again, and I sink down in my chair.

During the next lesson, the boy decides to throw things at me when the teacher isn't looking. It makes me feel sick and afraid to go to lunch with the others. So I try to find a quiet place to sit and eat my food, my meal fills up my tummy and makes me feel better for a while. I wish I didn't have to go back to class, but maybe we will do some maths today, that would cheer me up I think.

At lunchtime, I draw in the dirt with a stick for something to do. I like to draw shapes and patterns because I'm not very good at pictures, my friend Asad is though. I wish he were here to draw with me. We usually draw together every day after we have eaten.

When we go back to our classroom after lunch, the teacher tells us we are all going to write a letter to our pen pals. We know a class of students just like us who live in America, and we send letters back and forth. It helps us to practice our English writing, and it is fun to make new friends. My pen pal is named Sarah, so I write her a letter and tell her about my day, I decide to tell her about my walk to school and how I enjoyed the time away from my family. I miss my family now though because I feel lonely. So when we turn in our letters, I rush straight home. The air is hot, and the sky is very clear,

so it makes me tried to walk so fast under the hot sun.

"Hello Waleed," my oldest sister says when I get home.

"Hi," I reply.

"What's wrong did you have a bad day?" she asks.

"I had the worst day at school," I tell her "Asad wasn't there and there was a boy making fun of me all day."

"That's no good, little brother, why don't we make some tea and you can tell me all about it?" she asks.

I nod and come to the kitchen to heat the water. My sister always knows how to make me feel better. She pours me a cup of hot tea, and I carry it to the table to sit down.

"Why so sad?" she asks.

"Well, I was really excited to go to school this morning, but then I realized I had forgotten my drink bottle, and then Asad didn't come, and then a boy laughed at me because I couldn't read the book properly," I say.

"That was mean of him, I think you are very brave for reading aloud in front of the class," she tells me.

"Then he started throwing things at me, but I got to write a letter to Sarah after lunch. I was feeling lonely, so I came straight home," I say.

"That's good, I'm sure she will really like your letter! Asad will probably be back at school tomorrow, and then you will feel better again," she says, and I think she is probably right.

"Thank you for talking with me," I say, "I love you."

"I love you too, Waleed," she says and finishes her tea.

I stay at the table to finish mine, and our 5 siblings come home from their school. They are younger than us so they go to different classes. They all come back laughing and playing games, it makes me feel better to see them. I can't help but smile when they run over and hug me. It makes me feel happier to be around people who are so fun.

Worst Day At School

It was a warm Saturday morning, and Yousef was getting

excited. He was in the car on the way to the airport for an exciting adventure. Yousef and his family were going to Italy for a holiday! Yousef had been to Italy before, but he was so small he could not remember it at all. This time, he was ten and would remember the trip forever. His dad was driving the car down the long roads, and his mother was singing along to the radio. Yousef was staring out of the window watching the other cars go by.

When they arrived at the airport, they unloaded their bags and put them on a special trolley, Yousef's father pushed the cart all the way to the waiting room. They had to show their passports and tickets at the desk. Yousef memorized the seat numbers for the plane and was very excited to get to his seat. It was a long plane ride, and Yousef watched the land look so small out of the windows, he also watched some movies in the special TV. His mum took a nap but Yousef was much too excited to sleep, he was thinking about all of the fun things he would get to do on holiday.

When they arrived in Italy, it was late in the day, and the family traveled straight to the hotel where they would stay. Yousef loved the big soft bed he had to sleep in and the big tv to watch, but most of all he loved the view of the busy street and all the bright colors he could see. Yousef was excited to go exploring, they had a lot planned for their big adventure, like eating yummy food, going on tours, and visiting interesting places. They would be away from home for two whole weeks!

"Get your coat," his mum called, "we are going to go and get dinner!"

"Coming!" said Yousef, and rushed to find his things, "where are we going?"

"There's a nice restaurant down the street," said his dad, and they started walking.

Yousef could smell the food before they walked into the building, and he realized he was very hungry. A fancy looking waiter took them to a table and gave them menus. Yousef ordered a big bowl of spaghetti with lots of cheese on top, and for dessert he

ordered gelato. The food was delicious and made them all very happy.

The next day Yousef and his mum and dad went on a tour of the town they were staying in. It was a very special tour because they got to ride on electric scooters! Yousef was even allowed to drive his own, and he had a lot of fun. They learned a lot about the old buildings, they had been built over one hundred years ago and belonged to wealthy people. Yousef imagined what it would be like to be rich and live in a big fancy house.

"If I were rich like them, I'd live with all my friends, and instead of going to school we would play video games," Yousef told his father.

"That sounds like a lot of fun!" his dad said.

"Will you teach me to play video games so I can live there too?" asked his mum.

"Yes!" said Yousef, and they kept going along the streets listening to the stories.

The day after their scooter tour Yousef's mum and dad took him to a city called Venice, this was Yousef's favorite place. He liked it so much because instead of roads there were big canals full of water and instead of cars they had boats. At the back of the boat, a man would stand and paddle along for you, Yousef learned these boats were called 'gondolas.' On this day Yousef went on lots of gondola rides and saw lots of people dressed up in masks and colorful costumes. Yousef thought it would be so much fun to dress up just like them. They would perform songs and dances for him, and Yousef enjoyed it very much.

"Can I buy one of those masks to take home and show my friends?" Yousef asked.

"That's a wonderful idea," said his mum, and took him to choose a mask.

She helped him count the money, and Yousef chose a red mask with lots of feathers on it. Yousef loved the soft feathers and couldn't wait to show his friends at school and tell them all about the performers he had seen.

Another fun activity Yousef got to do on his holiday was to learn how to make pizza! They took a special pizza making class where Yousef learned all about the process. First, he learned how to make the dough, and kneaded it on the bench. Then the chef showed the class how to toss the dough, and spin it very fast until it became a big circle. Yousef's mother dropped her dough on the floor and Yousef, and his father laughed at her. Next was Yousef's turn, he did quite well, and made a small circle shape. The chef put his pizza onto a tray, and Yousef got to put his favorite toppings on it. He chose tomato paste, pepperoni, mushrooms, capsicum, and lots and lots of yummy cheese!

"Now we will put the pizzas in the oven!" said the chef.

"I can't wait to eat my pizza!" said Yousef.

"It looks delicious," said his mum and they went and sat down at a table. Yousef watched his pizza cook in the big oven until it was ready to eat! The chef brought it out to them and chopped it into slices.

"Enjoy your beautiful pizza!" He said with a big smile. Yousef did lots of fun things on his big holiday to Italy, and he was sad when he had to get on the plane to go back home.

"Can we come to Italy again one day?" he asked his parents.

"Of course!" said his mother.

"I think that would be wonderful," said his dad.

Welcome Home

Ahmed opened his eyes just as the bus was pulling into the station. He had arrived in Amman, the beautiful capital city of Jordan. Ahmed rubbed his eyes and stretched his arms. The two-hour bus ride from his hometown of Al Karak had been pleasant, and Ahmed had soon fallen asleep. Picking up his suitcase, Ahmed climbed off the bus and stepped into the crowd. There were people everywhere, and Ahmed tightened his grip on his bag. Spotting a taxi sign, he made his way toward the line of waiting taxis and got into the first one.

"Where to sir?" asked the taxi driver. "I would like to go to the Jordan Tower Hotel please" Ahmed answered.

The taxi started to drive into the busy city of Amman, and Ahmed looked out the window in amazement. He could not believe there were so many people and so much traffic. All around him, he could hear the horns of cars and buses, people shouting and children laughing. This city was very different from his hometown.

After a short 15-minute ride, the taxi pulled up outside the hotel. Ahmed paid the driver and took his luggage into the lobby. The receptionist found his reservation and showed him up to his room. It was a small, but clean room. Ahmed put down his luggage and sat down on the bed, it had been a long day for him. He felt his mobile phone start to vibrate and ring. He pulled it from his pocket and answered it: "Hello?"

"Hello Ahmed, it is Mr. Bashir, the landlord from the apartment you are coming to see tomorrow," said the voice on the other end.

"Oh yes! Hello Mr. Bashir, how can I help you?" asked Ahmed.

"I wanted to confirm with you that we are meeting outside the apartment in the morning at 11 o'clock", said Mr. Bashir.

"Yes, I will be there! See you then".

Ahmed hung up the phone. He was excited to start his new life in Amman. A new job and a new city. But first, he would need to organize himself a place to live.

Ahmed woke early the next morning, feeling irritated and hungry. He was annoyed because the traffic outside his hotel was so loud, and hungry because he fell asleep early the night before and missed out on dinner. Ahmed got up and showered, then made his way down to the lobby restaurant. He chose a table next to the window and sat down. A waiter with a friendly face approached him with a menu.

"Good morning sir! Can I offer you some coffee to start with?" asked the waiter.

"Yes please!" said Ahmed.

While the waiter hurried away, Ahmed looked through the

menu. He wanted a simple, yet satisfying breakfast, so when the waiter came back with his coffee, he ordered labneh with olive oil, za'atar, and flatbread.

With a full belly, Ahmed headed off to the apartment to meet the landlord. It was only a short 20-minute walk from the hotel, and it was a lovely day. The sun was shining, the air was sharp, and Ahmed felt alive.

As he was walking, Ahmed took his phone out of his pocket and dialed his brother's number, Ali. Samra, Ali's youngest daughter, answered the phone. "Uncle!" shouted Samra. Smiling, Ahmed started telling her all about his trip to Amman and what the big city was like. She listened, chiming in every now and then with a "wow!"

Again, this made Ahmed smile, picturing Samra's wide eyes and open mouth.

After a brief chat, Samra told Ahmed that her father had gone to the markets and had left his phone at home. Promising Samra to return the following month for her seventh birthday celebrations, Ahmed said goodbye. Ahmed loved his nieces and nephews and hoped to one day have children of his own.

In the distance, he could see a short, round man leaning against his car, waiting outside a large apartment block. "Ah, that must be Mr. Bashir," thought Ahmed. Taking in the view of the property, Ahmed was impressed. It didn't look too old but also didn't look brand new, which Ahmed liked.

"You must be Ahmed!" said Mr. Bashir, extending his hand.

"Yes! Nice to meet you", taking his hand and shaking it.

"Well, follow me. The apartment is on the third floor, so I hope you don't mind stairs!" remarked Mr. Bashir.

Climbing the stairs, Ahmed could feel the heat in the air. He hoped that it would be easier once the weather cooled down a little. Mr. Bashir led him to a door with the number 33 on it and opened it. They stepped inside the apartment and into a bright living area. There was a small, yet well-equipped kitchen to the right and a charming balcony overlooking the street below.

"This apartment is really perfect for what you are looking for Ahmed. It is in a fantastic location, very central and the price is within your budget", explained Mr. Bashir.

Ahmed had to agree with the landlord, as he walked around the flat. It was charming and not too small. He had a good feeling about it.

"I'll take it!" exclaimed Ahmed.

"Fantastic! So, the rental price is 315 Dinars per month, like I previously told you. And utilities should cost around 50 Dinars per month."

"Yes, that is no problem," said Ahmed, quickly calculating the total sum of 365 Dinars in his head.

"Well good! I am happy to rent this apartment to you. You can move in tomorrow, I will meet you here in the morning at 9 o'clock with the keys. Let me find the lease here in my briefcase."

While Mr. Bashir was rummaging around in his bag, Ahmed stepped out onto the balcony. He could smell the city. So many different aromas were floating all around him. There was so much life around him, and Ahmed was feeling very grateful he had the opportunity to live in Amman. This was going to be a new adventure for him.

After signing the lease, Mr. Bashir led Ahmed out of the apartment and down the stairs, before saying goodbye. With the afternoon free to explore, and only a stone's throw away from his hotel, Ahmed thought he would check out his new neighborhood.

Making a left turn from the apartment building, he found himself in a leafy tree-lined street, with lots of little stores and cafés. Wandering slowly down the road, he stopped outside a juice bar that had a little area to sit outside. Taking a seat, he was suddenly very thirsty. Back in Al Karak, the juice bar in his village was known to be the best in town.

"Let's see how Amman matches up," thought Ahmed. Ordering an orange juice, he took his first sip, the sun beating down on his head. For the first time since he had arrived, Ahmed was feeling

relaxed and happy.

A ball rolled towards him, and when Ahmed looked up, he could see a group of young boys standing nearby in a circle. Picking up the ball, Ahmed threw it back to the group. One of the boys caught the ball and called out "thank you!"

"Do you live here sir?" asked the boy.

For a moment, Ahmed had to think about it. But then, with a smile on his face, he answered: "yes, I live here."

Goal

"Pass me the ball Mohammed!" yelled Waleed from across the other side of the field.

Mohammed was so close to the goal posts, and he knew he had this goal in the bag.

Dribbling the ball in front of him, with the utmost concentration, Mohammed could hear his heart beating loudly in his ears. Ignoring all the calls from his teammates, Mohammed kicked the ball as hard as he could. Goal! The roar from the sidelines erupted, and Mohammed felt the adrenaline surge through his body. His teammates were all rallying around him, cheering and lifting him up into the air. Mohammed felt good. His team had won, and it was because of him.

Back in the change rooms, Mohammed's teammates kept patting him on the back and congratulating him. The door to the locker room opened and in walked the team's coach, Mr. Safik.

"Well done out there today Mohammed! You were fantastic", Mr. Safik said, shaking Mohammed's hand.

"In fact, so good, that the soccer club wants to send you on a soccer scholarship to go and play in England next year."

The rest of the team went silent, and Mohammed's mouth dropped open.

"What? Me? Going to live in England?" asked Mohammed.

"Yes! Of course, you will have to take English classes for the remainder of the year at an immersion school, but that shouldn't be

a problem for you", said the coach.

Beep beep! The alarm was going off. Today was his first class at the language immersion school. Mohammed could speak a tiny bit of English but was nowhere near ready to live in an English-speaking country.

The bus ride to the language school was around 20 minutes from his apartment. They pulled up outside a huge red-brick building. There were students everywhere, rushing around. Mohammed made his way to the reception. A friendly looking woman with blonde hair was sitting behind the desk.

"Hi there! How can I help you?" she asked in fast spoken English.

"Hello. My name is Mohammed..." Mohammed slowly said back.

Sensing that this was a new student, the woman smiled kindly and adjusted the speed of her talking. "Hello, Mohammed. My name is Lisa, welcome to Amman's immersion language school. Let me show you to your class".

Understanding only half of what Lisa had said, Mohammed nodded and followed her down a long corridor. She led him to a classroom, with a dozen students sitting inside at desks.

"Rosa, this is Mohammed. He is a new student, a Jordanian national."

Rosa, a large woman with a big smile, bustled over.

"Hello, Mohammed! Welcome to this class. Please take a seat at one of the desks", Rosa said, pointing to the tables.

Mohammed thanked Lisa and walked over to a desk next to the wall. He put his bag down and sat in the chair. Glancing around, Mohammed saw that all the other students looked Arab too. He looked over at the desk next to him where another boy was sitting. The boy smiled at him and stuck his hand out.

"Hi, I'm Omran," the man said in Arabic.

"Hey, I'm Mohammed. Nice to meet you. Although I'm fairly sure we are meant to speak in English?" asked Mohammed.

Omran laughed. "Yes, probably. But sometimes it is so much easier to speak in our native tongue!"

An hour into the lesson, Mohammed felt his concentration wane. It was so difficult. Everything was in English! If they wanted to ask a question, they had to ask it in English. Everything Rosa said was in English. Mohammed needed to use the bathroom. What was the difference between 'where' and 'who'? He raised his hand in the air.

"Yes Mohammed?" said Rosa.

"Um, who is the toilet"? asked Mohammed.

The class erupted into soft snickers, and Mohammed felt his face going red. He quickly glanced at his new friend, who simply looked at Mohammed with a sympathetic smile.

"I think you mean 'where' Mohammed, not 'who' but good try! The toilets are outside the classroom and at the end of the hall", said Rosa, pointing to the left. When Mohammed returned, they had to pair off and complete an exercise – introducing themselves. Mohammed was partnered with Omran, which he was happy about.

"Ok, I'll start," said Omran in Arabic.

"Hello. My name is Omran. I am 26-years old, and I am a student at the University of Amman. I study Engineering. I am single, and I love soccer", Omran said, in slow, but perfect English.

"Wow, you're good! How long have you been learning for?" asked Mohammed in Arabic.

Rosa heard the boys and came over. "Guys, please stick with English. I know it is hard, but at this language school, English is the only language spoken inside the classes to help you learn faster".

"Sorry," both the men said.

"Ok. My name is Mohammed. I am ... 28-years..."

"Old," prompted Omran.

"Yes. Old. I play soccer ... my club is sending me to England ... for scholarship".

"Really! That is awesome!" exclaimed Omran.

"Awesome?" asked Mohammed.

"Yes, awesome is something you say when something is great."

"Ohh yes," said Mohammed. He had heard that word used a few

times in American movies.

Later that night, Mohammed was exhausted, lying in bed. Learning another language definitely made you tired, he thought. He decided to watch an American movie on Netflix, with English subtitles.

Mohammed chose American Pie and pressed play. Half-way through the movie, he felt his brain feel foggy. He had to stop, this was information overload. It was hard to keep up with reading the subtitles and what they were saying in English. Nevertheless, he vowed to watch a movie every night, with English sub-titles until he had mastered the language.

A month passed, and Mohammed had been attending the language school every day for 3 hours. He was already surprised at how much he had learned in that short space of time.

"Ok, everyone! Are we ready today for our 'short dialogue' presentations?" asked Rosa.

"Mohammed, you can go first."

Mohammed got up and walked to the front of the class. He was ready for this, he had been practicing for the last week, and he had memorized it.

"Hello. I'm Mohammed. I am 28-years old, and I work at a restaurant. I love to play soccer, and my club is sending me to England on a scholarship next year. I have never been to England. I think I will like it. I have one older brother and one younger sister. I live 20 minutes from this language school. My favorite food is falafel, and my favorite drink is coffee. I would like to learn English so I can make friends in England. Maybe I can even find a wife there".

The class, including Rosa, laughed.

"Well done Mohammed! That was excellent. Ok, does anyone have any questions for Mohammed?"

A woman at the front raised her hand. "Mohammed, what is your position in soccer?" Mohammed knew this one. "I am left midfield. But I would like to be a goalkeeper too".

"Great!" said Rosa. "Any other questions?"

A man at the back raised his hand. "How long will you live in England for?"

"One year."

"Ok, one more question," said Rosa.

Omran called out "Mohammed, what is the best thing you have done this year?"

Mohammed grinned. "Learning to speak English."

Oh, Doctor

The air was warm, and the lights on the river were shining. The conversation was flowing, the food and drinks were delicious, and the shisha was even better. Omar looked around at this group of friends, all sitting in a circle, having a good night.

"But seriously Omar, when do you think you will get married?" asked his best friend, Ibrahim.

Omar scrunched up a napkin and threw it at him.

"Not anytime soon! I am young! Not even 28. I want to make sure I marry the right woman, and I don't think I have met her yet", replied Omar.

His friends laughed and nodded. They understood. In fact, only one man out of the group was married. He had met his wife quite young, at the age of 19.

A waiter arrived with a fresh shisha and hot coals. Omar knew it wasn't healthy for him, but he did love to smoke a good shisha once in a while.

Needing to use the bathroom, Omar stood up and walked inside the restaurant. All of a sudden, a door swung open from the left side of the hall and struck Omar.

"Ouch!" cried Omar, falling backward.

"I am so sorry! That was an accident! This stupid bathroom door was stuck so I had to give it a hard push", said a woman.

Omar looked up at the woman, and for a second, he felt his heart stop beating. She was beautiful. Her green eyes were large

and sincere, as she offered Omar a hand up. Omar grabbed her hand and hoisted himself up.

"Oh, that's fine. Don't worry about it. These things happen", said Omar.

"Are you sure you are alright? I feel terrible knocking a grown man to the ground", said the woman.

"Yes, yes. I am fine. Hi, I am Omar. Nice to... meet you!"

The woman laughed, and Omar swore he could see her blushing.

"Hi Omar, I'm Noora. Again, I am sorry about before. I hope you have a good rest of the evening". And with that, she turned around and left.

Omar walked into the bathroom and caught himself in the mirror. He looked sheepish. What a gorgeous woman, he thought.

Omar woke up the next morning with a terrible feeling in his throat. It felt raw like someone was scraping their nails along it every time he swallowed. Omar felt awful. He must have had too much to smoke last night, he thought.

He got up and went into the bathroom, he opened his mouth wide and looked in the mirror.

'Uh-oh,' he thought. 'This doesn't look good.' His throat was inflamed and very red. 'Surely this can't just come from smoking shisha.'

Omar sighed and picked up his phone to make an appointment with his doctor.

"Hi doctor, this is Omar Sayeed. I need to come in and see you, my throat is very sore, and I need you to take a look at it".

"Omar! Yes, you may come in, but I am leaving early today so one of the other doctors will have to see you instead".

"That's fine doctor – can I come in this afternoon?"

"Yes, I will make an appointment for you. Bye Omar". Omar flicked through an old magazine in the waiting room. Why was it that doctor's waiting rooms always had old magazines in it, he thought to himself.

"Omar Sayeed?" said a woman's voice.

Omar put the magazine back down on the table and stood up. Standing in front of him, calling his name was ... the woman from the other night, Noora!

"Follow me please Omar," she said, turning around and leading him to her office. He followed her into the room and sat down on the patient's chair, while Noora sat at her desk.

"Noora? Wow, what a surprise. You're a doctor?"

"Yes, I am. What a small world! I hope you did not come in today because of your fall last night?" Noora asked.

"Oh! No! I am here because..." Omar trailed off. Suddenly he felt a little shy and foolish.

Omar liked this woman. Was he really going to sit here and open his mouth for her to look into?

"Yes? Go ahead, Omar."

"Well, I woke up this morning with a burning throat, and it looks quite inflamed to me," said Omar.

"Ok. Any other symptoms? A headache? Nasal congestion? Fever?"

"No, but I don't feel great. A little hot I suppose." Noora picked up a throat stick and walked around the other side of the desk.

"Open your mouth please and say 'ahh.'"

Omar tilted his head back and opened his mouth. He felt silly.

Noora pressed the throat stick against his tongue and had a look.

"Hmm, right. Your tonsils are quite inflamed. Looks to me like a general case of tonsillitis. You will need to take antibiotics for it to clear up".

"Okay sure, thanks for checking it out for me," said Omar.

"Of course! I am a doctor. That is my job".

Omar felt himself go red.

"You will also need to rinse your mouth and gargle with salt water, to help the pain and swelling."

"Let's check inside your ears too," Noora said as she shone a torch into them.

"They look fine to me. I will take your temperature". Noora

grabbed a thermometer from her desk and told Omar to stick it under his armpit.

"How long have you been a doctor for?" he asked.

"This is my third year as a practicing doctor. I graduated when I was still quite young".

"May I ask how old you are? Or is that rude?" asked Omar. Noora giggled. "I am 29".

"Oh! Only a couple years older than myself" exclaimed Omar. Just bite the bullet, he thought. She is a beautiful, intelligent woman. It was no accident that you bumped into her at the restaurant last night and now today.

"Um, Doctor Noora. This may be highly inappropriate of me, but, I was wondering if you would like to have a coffee with me once I am better? I know I don't know you, but I couldn't help but notice how beautiful you were when you, umm, accidentally hit me with the door last night. And you seem like such a nice person, I would really like to get to know you a little better. If you want?"

Omar realized he was babbling and that he still had the thermometer under his armpit. It started beeping, so he took it out.

Noora smiled. "You have a slight temperature, but that is because your body has an infection. And yes Omar. I would like to have coffee with you. Now go and rest up."

Omar thanked her as she handed him his prescriptions and left the office.

He hated being sick, but this, he thought, was definitely a silver lining.

He went to the reception desk and paid his fee of 30 Dinars. Fortunately, there was a pharmacy next door, so he handed in his prescriptions and waited.

The pharmacist was an older man. "Omar Sayeed?" he called.

"Yes," Omar stepped forward.

"Ok, you need to take these antibiotics twice a day, after you eat, for a week. If you are not getting better, please go back and see Doctor...", the pharmacist was looking at the prescription. "Ah,

Noora! Lovely lady, isn't she?".

Omar smiled. "She is."

A Golden Opportunity

Randa had been working for the banking company for five years, and she was a star employee. She was always on time, worked more than the hours required, and her colleagues loved her. She was definitely an asset to the company. Which is why it should have been no surprise when she was called into her boss's office one morning and was offered the opportunity to go and work for the bank's head office in New York.

"You want me to go and live and work in New York?" Randa asked her boss, Noora.

"Yes, Randa. An opportunity has opened up, and we think you would be perfect for the job. You are excellent at what you do, and we want to open a new door for you – if you would like it", said Noora.

It wasn't that Randa wouldn't like it, but she was afraid. It would mean leaving Jordan, her family, and friends and moving to a foreign country where she knew no one. Her English was okay, but she would definitely need to pick up some classes before she moved.

"I… don't know what to say Noora. I am very grateful for being considered for this opportunity. But I don't think I can give you a definite answer right now", said Randa.

"That's fine Randa. Take your time, we don't have to give head office an official response until the end of the week".

It was Tuesday. Randa had three days to think about this huge decision. She thanked Noora and left her office.

Sitting back down at her desk, Randa tried to take it all in. She texted her best friend, Aisha.

"Are you free tonight after work? Usual coffee house spot?", texted Randa. Her phone buzzed two minutes later. "Sure, see you then Ran."

Randa could see Aisha, sitting at their spot in the corner of the

coffee house, with two cups of tea in front of her. Randa rushed in and sat down.

"Thanks for meeting me Aiash!"

"No problem girl. Are you okay?" asked Aisha.

Randa took a deep breath. She knew Aisha wasn't going to like this news.

"My work has asked me if I would like to transfer to the head office in New York." Aisha was silent. Just staring at Randa."And... I don't know if I want to take the opportunity or not".

"Wow Ran. This is huge! First of all, congratulations for even getting the offer. Second of all, don't go", said Aisha.

The girls both fell into a fit of laughter.

"I'm serious! Don't leave me! You are my best friend. What will I do here without you?" asked Aisha.

"I know. I really don't know what to do. On the one hand, I have my family and friends here. But on the other hand, how cool would it be to live in America! New York even. It wouldn't be forever. It would just be temporary", said Randa.

"Yeah, that's what they all say. And then they end up married to Americans, have babies and boom, they never move back to Jordan".

"Don't say that. I want to have a family here, in Amman. But I am also 27. I want to experience what the world has to offer me", reasoned Randa.

Aisha could see that her friend was torn. What would she do if she were in that position, she thought. She would definitely be tempted to go, even if it meant leaving everything behind here.

"I am going to have to talk to my parents tonight. Baba will know what to do, he always does", said Randa.

Later that night, as Randa sat at the dinner table with her parents and younger sister, she cleared her throat. Her family looked at her.

"I have something to tell you all," said Randa.

"Oh! You've met a man! You are getting married! Thank god, the day has finally come!" cried her mother.

"Shh, Lina. Let our daughter speak", said her father.

"Um, actually no. I have been offered a position with my work to move to the head office in New York", said Randa.

Lina's face fell.

"What! No! Are you kidding? Why do they think they can do that? Don't they know you have a family here? You have no family in America! What silly people!" cried Lina, again.

"Well, this is my predicament. I don't know what to do", said Randa. She looked at her sister, who was looking at her, smiling.

"What do you mean you don't know what to do? You can't go! We need you here. You need to meet a nice Jordanian boy and get married and have a family. You are already 27 years old. I was married with two children by your age! Ali, say something!" yelled Lina.

Randa's father, Ali, was taking it all in. His face looked thoughtful as if he was processing all the information and already weighing up the pros and cons.

"Randa. Do you want to move to America and take this position?" asked Ali.

"I don't know, baba. I think I do, but I am also afraid", said Randa.

"Ali! Randa!" screeched Lina. She stood up from the table and stormed out of the room.

"Just give her time Randa," said Ali. "She loves you very much, so it is hard for her to imagine you not living here anymore."

"I think you should go," piped up Randa's sister, Amina.

"Really?" asked Randa.

"Yes! This is a fantastic opportunity for you Ran. For your career and also... for your life! You can always come back to Jordan, but for now, do this while you still can!" said Amina.

"I have to agree with your sister. As much as we will miss you, moving to America is a fantastic opportunity for you", said Ali.

Randa had a lot to think about.

The next day, Randa knocked on her boss's office door.

"Randa, come in!" said Noora. Randa went in and sat down.

"Thanks, Noora. I have a few questions for you about my potential move to New York," said Randa.

"Sure, go ahead," said Noora, smiling.

"When would I need to move?" asked Randa.

"We will need you to start at the beginning of the month, so in three weeks", answered Noora. Three weeks? Okay, that was viable, thought Randa.

"Ok. And will I be getting a pay raise?" asked Randa.

"Oh yes! I thought I told you this yesterday, but perhaps it slipped my mind. You will be getting a significant pay increase, plus a yearly bonus and the company will pay for your rent in New York. You will be looked after very well", replied Noora.

"Oh! Yes, this certainly makes a difference", said Randa.

"Really Randa, this is an amazing opportunity for a young woman like yourself. You would be foolish to turn it down. I moved to America, Los Angeles actually, when I was your age, and it was the best thing I ever did. I lived there for two years and learned more about myself than I thought possible. I met a Jordanian man over there, so we ended up moving back to Amman, but I am so grateful for those two years", said Noora.

Randa smiled. It was going to be challenging, and her mother certainly wasn't going to like it. But Randa wanted to grow, and she wanted to better herself.

Her mind was made up. She knew what she had to do.

Bad Luck

Cycling to work, Leena's legs hurt. It was an eight-kilometer ride one-way from her apartment to her office in the center of Amman. She was halfway there, but yesterday she had been to the gym and today, her whole body ached. Pushing through it, Leena grimaced and kept pedaling. 'I wish I could afford a car, any car will do' thought Leena.

Leena arrived at work. As she was locking her bike up, her boss walked past her.

"Good morning Leena! That must be good exercise for you!" said her boss, Ahmed.

"Hello, Ahmed. Yes, you could say that. But I think I am ready for a car. I have been riding a bike for the last 20 years of my life. If I have to ride through another winter...". Ahmed smiled at her sympathetically and went inside.

Later that day, while Leena was in the tea room, Ahmed wandered in. He came over to her, and in a hushed tone, he asked "Leena, I have been thinking about what you said this morning, about you wanting a car. And well, my wife is actually selling her car because she is buying a new one. It is quite an old car, but it runs very well and it still reliable. She is selling it for a cheap price. Would you be interested?"

"Ohh. Thank you for thinking of me Ahmed! May I ask how much she is selling it for?" asked Leena, concerned about the price.

"Only 2000 Dinars. But I am sure we could knock off another couple hundred of Dinars for you. Let me speak to my wife."

"Great, thanks Ahmed, let me know."

Delighted, Leena returned to her desk. That price was definitely affordable for her, she had already saved 2500 Dinars for a car but had not been able to find anything decent for that price. Before Leena left for work that day, Ahmed sent her an email. It read:

'Hi, Leena. I spoke to my wife earlier, and she has agreed to sell you the car for 1,800 Dinars. Does this work for you? If so, I can arrange to bring the car in tomorrow to work for you. If you could pay via bank transfer, that would be great. Let me know. Thanks, Ahmed.'

Leena wrote back:

'Hi Ahmed, that sounds great! Please let your wife know I would love to buy the car from her. I will transfer her the money tomorrow. Thanks again Ahmed, this is a big help! Leena'. Leena arrived at work the next morning bright and early. She had caught a cab to work. It was such a nice feeling knowing she would not have to cycle into work anymore.

Leena walked towards the back of the building and saw Ahmed pulling into the car park in a slightly older, but still nice looking car. He got out and saw her.

"She's all yours!" exclaimed Ahmed, jingling the keys in the air.

Leena clasped her hands together joyfully. She walked over to the car and opened the driver's door. She got inside and sat in the seat. It smelt like perfume. It was a little old inside (the car was made in 2001), but Leena decided it had a nice look to it.

"I love it, Ahmed. I will transfer the money into your wife's account today. Please email me the details" said Leena.

For the next two weeks, Leena drove everywhere in her car. She loved having such freedom, driving to her parents' place in the west and visiting her sister in the east. She and a friend even went all the way to the beach one weekend.

One morning, on her way to work, Leena was stuck in the usual Amman peak hour traffic. Slowly inching along, stopping and starting, Leena heard a funny noise. It was almost as if her car was grunting at her. Suddenly, the car jerked forward and stopped, abruptly in the middle of the traffic. Leena jiggled the keys in the ignition to turn it back on, but it wouldn't start. It just kept making this hissing sound. 'Oh no' thought Leena. 'What am I going to do?' The cars behind her were all honking their horns. Feeling panicked, Leena turned her head around and could see a long line of cars. 'What do I do! Wait... remember that time your father's car broke down when you were younger. What did he do... that's right! He put the hazard lights on'.

Leena searched for the red button with a triangle on it. She pressed it, and the car's indicators both came on. 'Ok, now what?' She got out of the car and shrugged her shoulders the cars behind her. A man in one of the vehicles hopped out and came over.

"Has your car broken down miss?" he asked her.

"Yes! What should I do?" she asked him back.

"Get back in the car. I am going to push it, and I want you to steer the car to the side of the road".

Leena got back in, as the man started to push the back of her car. She steered the wheel towards the side of the road, and it slowly began to move. Finally, once the car was off the road, traffic rushed past her.

She got out again. "Thank you, sir. My brother is a mechanic. I will call him".

The man smiled and waved, got back into his car and drove away.

Leena pulled her phone out of her bag and dialed in her brother, Jamal's number. "Hi Jamal. I need your help. My 'new' car has broken down on the side of the highway" said Leena.

"Really? That is bad luck! Text me exactly where you are, and I will try and be there in 30 minutes" said Jamal.

Leena texted Jamal and then called her office. The receptionist picked up the phone.

"Hi Mara, it's Leena. My car has broken down on the way to work so I will be late today".

"Hi, Leena. I am sorry to hear that. Thanks for calling and letting me know, I will pass this message onto Ahmed" said the receptionist.

Leena waited. Jamal was right, this definitely was bad luck. She had only purchased the car two weeks ago! Maybe Leena needed to have the car serviced. She should have had the car checked before she bought it, she thought.

A car started beeping. It was Jamal. He pulled over behind her car.

"Thank god! Jamal, I have no idea what is wrong with this car!" cried Leena.

Jamal got out of his car. "Let's have a look'.

He walked around to the front of the car and opened the bonnet. He looked inside for about 10 minutes, tweaking things here and there.

"Leena, there seems to be a problem with the alternator."

'Whatever that means...' thought Leena.

"I am going to have to call my guys to tow the car back to the garage. We will work on it there. I'd say it will be with us for around

4 days."

The next day, as Leena rode her bike to work, she was actually grateful. Grateful for her bike and how trustworthy it was.

'At least this isn't going to break down!' thought Leena.

The Big Day

Noor had met Karim six months ago at a conference in Amman. To say it was 'love at first sight' would have been an understatement. Noor had never felt such a strong connection with another human being as she did with Karim. They were both doctors, and they both had a love of good food, the outdoors and Prince. He calmed her down, and she sparked his energy. So, when Karim proposed, Noor wasn't surprised, but she was very happy.

Being an Egyptian born in America, Karim was fairly new to the Jordanian customs and traditions, but he was more than happy to learn more and was excited to embark on this journey with Noor.

"Okay, so we have the engagement ceremony and dinner party next week – are you ready?" asked Noor.

Karim laughed. "I think so! How hard can it be?"

Noor went quiet. It's not that it was going to be 'hard,' but Noor did hope that Karim wouldn't become too overwhelmed. She could imagine that coming into a Jordanian family could be a little daunting. There were just so many family members and new cultural norms to get accustomed to. But she had no doubt Karim was up to the job. She was, after all, marrying the man.

The following Thursday, Noor and Karim arrived at Noor's parent's house. Her mother and father greeted them warmly, fussing over Karim. Traditionally, Karim's parents were meant to be there too, but since they were planning on getting married in Jordan, his parents were already coming over from America for that. They entered Noor's parent's house and went into the living room. Noor's sister, cousin and her best friend were there, as well as a couple of male friends of Karim's from work. They all greeted each other and Noor and her mother, Zara, took a seat on the couch

with the women and Karim and Noor's father, Mohammed, sat on another sofa with the men.

"Well, I am so glad we can all be here today for this informal gathering. Karim, Noor's mother and I would like to welcome you to the family. We are very excited to have a foreigner in our family!" laughed Mohammed.

The rest of the group laughed too, and Noor looked over at Karim and winked.

Karim cleared his throat.

"Thank-you Mohammed and Zara. I am very excited to be marrying your daughter, she makes me very happy", said Karim, looking over at Noor and smiling. Noor smiled back. "I would like to formally ask you both for permission to marry Noor," said Karim.

Noor's parents both smiled and nodded at Karim.

Pulling a small box from his pocket, Karim presented Noor with a traditional engagement gift. Noor accepted the gift and opened the box. It was a pair of beautiful diamond earrings. "Thank-you Karim, I love them!" said Noor.

They both then exchanged engagement rings – simple gold bands – and put them on each other's second middle fingers on their right hands.

"Congratulations you two! Now, let's eat!" cried Mohammed. Noor turned to the women, who all hugged and kissed her. Her mother squeezed her hard.

"Who would have thought my baby daughter would be married before her big sister!" she exclaimed, glancing over at Fatima, Noor's sister.

Fatima smiled sweetly at her mother, "I guess Noor met her Mr. Right before I did mother!"

They all gathered at the dining table, where a spread of food was awaiting them. There was falafel, hummus, labneh, tabbouleh, salad, and a range of meats, rice, and sweets. They ate and laughed, and by the end of dinner, Karim was feeling like part of the family.

A whirlwind four months passed and Noor finally woke on the

day of her wedding. She had butterflies in her stomach. Her sister and friends would be arriving shortly to help her get ready. She rose and went and had a shower.

Meanwhile, on the other side of town, Karim was doing the same thing. His friends would be arriving soon too. His parents had flown in two nights ago and were staying at a hotel in the city, close to the restaurant where the wedding reception was taking place. Some of his friends from home had also come to Jordan for the big day. He was excited to see everyone.

That afternoon, both bride and groom arrived at Noor's parent's house. The house was glowing from all the lights that had been draped on the outside of the building. It was an Arab tradition, and it looked very impressive. Noor's family and friends were seated on one side of the living room and Karim's family and friends on the other side. Karim sat facing everyone. Arabic music was playing, and sweets were being offered to all the guests. Suddenly, the music stopped, and traditional wedding tunes started instead.

Noor and her father entered the room and sat down. Karim silently gasped. He had never seen Noor look so beautiful. Once the signing of the legal documents had taken place, Karim came over to Noor and kissed her on the head. They both moved each other's rings from the right hand to their second middle fingers on their left hands.

After the ceremony, all the guests headed to the restaurant for the reception. Noor and Karim stayed behind.

"Wow! It's done! How do you feel Karim?" asked Noor.

"I thought it was lovely. You look stunning", said Karim, as he leaned in to kiss her.

Noor wanted this moment to last forever, but she also knew they were on a schedule. They got into the car that was waiting for them out the front of the house. On the way to the restaurant, Karim held Noor's hand.

"I am so glad I ended up at that conference and decided to take

the position at the Amman hospital. It has all led me to you", said Karim.

Noor's heart felt so full, as if it might burst then and there!

They arrived at the restaurant, which was very fancy. It had high ceilings and floors made from marble. The décor was cream, and all the fittings were made out of rose gold. They headed inside, and everyone started cheering. Their friends and family were all sitting at round tables, and the music had already begun. The food and drinks were flowing, and a dance floor had been set up. Noor and Karim were welcomed for their first dance together as husband and wife. Karim took Noor into his arms, and her favorite Arabic song started to play. They danced slowly, smiling at each other with such joy. When the song was over, everyone was invited onto the dance floor, and that's when the real fun began. Dance moves of all kind were being displayed, and everyone was having a ball.

Karim and Noor took a step back and watched all the people from their lives, dancing and enjoying life.

"Now this is a real celebration," said Karim. "Your family definitely know how to live life and put on a party."

Noor smiled.

She was pleased that it had all gone so well and that Karim seemed to fit into her life, family, and culture so easily.

She took his hand and squeezed it, excited for what the next chapter of their lives would bring them.

GET THE AUDIO

We hope you've enjoyed and benefited from **Egyptian Arabic: *Easy Stories With English Translations*** .

The audio for these stories and much more is available to listen to on our website at *www.talkinarabic.com*.